D1055238

Christopher's Summer

Christopher's Summer

A father and son explore the
MYSTERIES of LIFE and DEATH

Jeffrey S. Dugan

Illustrated by Mark J. Weisman

Cumberland House
Nashville, Tennessee

Copyright © 2001 by Jeffrey S. Dugan

Illustrations copyright © 2001 by Mark J. Weisman.
All rights reserved.

All rights reserved. Written permission must be secured
from the publisher to use or reproduce any part of this
work, except for brief quotations in critical reviews or
articles.

Published by Cumberland House Publishing, Inc.,
431 Harding Industrial Drive, Nashville, TN 37211
www.cumberlandhouse.com

Cover design by Becky Brawner

Library of Congress Cataloging-in-Publication Data
is available.
ISBN: 1-58182-239-1

Printed in the United States of America
1 2 3 4 5 6 7—06 05 04 03 02 01

To Matthew, Claire, Christopher,
and William: You are the light of my life
and the joy in my heart.

And for Dad
1933–2000

FOREWORD

The summer I was fourteen I went off with my grandparents to a lake resort in New England, not unlike the one where the Dugans you will meet in this book spend their vacation. My first day there I met a boy my age named Johnny, and I spent some time with him. Then, that afternoon, while I was playing baseball, he climbed a mountain with his sister, and at the summit, while sitting on a ledge, he suddenly pitched over and fell down the sheer rock face to his death. We could look up from the baseball field and see them trying to rescue him.

I wrote my parents about this in great detail, a letter which my mother saved and gave me years later, along with some other childhood memorabilia. I read over the letter now with morbid fascination. Johnny was really my first encounter with death, and I was obviously so shocked and confounded. I can see through my thoughts and my emotions in the letter. Nervously I would stop writing about the accident and tell about the baseball game or a pretty girl I had spied or how cold it was or this or that—but I would always go back to the boy who died on the mountain. Near the end of the letter I write:

"Johnny did not impress me as a boy who would be an everyday companion, but he seemed nice. I just keep thinking of him." And then I got to what was really on my mind: "He rode right next to me on the boat that morning. But for the grace of God it could have been me. Sometimes I just don't know how lucky I am."

I'm sure, till that moment, that it had never occurred to me that I might die—well, not until I was very, very old, an ancient, contented patriarch who would be quite ready to meet my maker. But instead, there it was: two boys riding in a boat side-by-side in the morning and one of them dead and gone that afternoon. And I was the boy who didn't die. I was the boy who was going to keep on living. But who could have known which one? Never again could I not at least consider death as a viable part of my world.

I imagine most children come at the reality that way. Death is sprung upon them in some intimate fashion. Maybe it is more complicated now that we see death so casually portrayed in the movies and on TV and in video *games*. But then, it used to be—and not all that long ago, either—that real death was quite commonplace in the home itself. Children got sick and, often as not, they died. It was a part of growing up, losing brothers or sisters. So maybe the ersatz death we watch today in entertainment is nothing but a substitute for how it truly was through eons of sad reality. Anyway, it's difficult enough for a child's mind to comprehend that finality. I even read once that a child simply cannot fathom the totality of death until something like the age of ten or eleven.

Certainly it is unusual for a happy, healthy child like Christopher Dugan to persist in asking about death. But then, other kids ask about things like how the e-mail gets in the computer even when it is turned off and how roller coasters go upside down without falling—and death is just another mystery in a world full of more and more of them. Christopher is not fey, just delightfully inquisitive. Also, Christopher knew his old man, the preacher, was supposed to be a professional expert in these matters. A kid likes to take advantage of his father's special wisdom. When my son was growing up, he would never have been so foolish as to ask me, the sportswriter, how a toaster oven works, but he would ask me to explain how a curve ball curves or how you get tickets for a big game.

So I think that you, as I, will be glad that Christopher presumed on his father's expertise, because Jeffrey's answers are both thoughtful and comforting. But they're not facile. I don't want to hear from anybody who is smug about the subject of dying.

No doubt this is especially true in my case, because I was not so lucky as to be able to deal with all my children with death in the abstract. My daughter, Alex, died of cystic fibrosis when she was eight years old. We could see it coming, and so, at last, could she. "I'm going home to die," she confided to her favorite nurse when she left the hospital for the last time, "but don't tell my parents, because it will upset them."

And so she did die and so it did upset us. But we didn't really know any more. Somebody else's dying doesn't really teach you about death. If you're lucky, you might, however, learn something about yourself, living on. Oh sure, we prepared ourselves for losing Alex, as best as we could—which is to say, not very well. And we tried to prepare Alex, too. Dying, for a child like Alex—or thinking about dying, for a child like Christopher—is all the more frightening, because children are not used to being on their own. As hard as it is for anyone to visualize heaven, still, for a child, it is surely easier to conjure up heaven than to imagine being there all by yourself.

So children have different questions, different urgencies about death and dying than we adults do, which makes it all the more revealing for us to be able to hear Jeffrey and Christopher talking together, father and son, man and boy. It's a wonderful colloquy we're privileged to listen in on.

—Frank Deford

ACKNOWLEDGMENTS

This book would not exist in its present form were it not for the support and advice I have received over the past three years from the following wonderful people: Caroline Andersen, Debbie Andersen, Emily Andersen, Martha Andersen, Jim and Katrina Byers, Abigail Crawford, Fred and Sharon DeHaven, Michael and Priscilla Dugan, Peter Dugan, Bert and Babs Findlay, Carl Hagelin, Lee Hagelin, Barbara and Steven Henricks, Sarah and Draper Hill, Josephine Ingram, Joan and Paul Ingram, Jane Inrig, Helene Kimball, Nancy Madway, Patricia Milliken, Jan Owens, Bob Patin, Art and Be Phinney, Rachael de Rham, Fred Rowland, Whit Shepard, Elizabeth Thornton, and Kurt Woodward. For their encouragement and honest feedback, I thank each and every one from the bottom of my heart.

In the earliest days of the manuscript's evolution, Annabel Stehli invested countless hours of her time giving me editing advice, offering her unflagging enthusiasm for the project, and sharing her wisdom of the publishing world. Verne and Barbara Blodgett offered me the quiet sanctuary of their beautiful home for important revision work on a few occasions, as well as their encouragement and sage advice throughout the past three years. Andrew Ackemann helped without even knowing it, through a story he told me years ago. Jane Garrett, of Knopf Publishing, gave critical publishing advice just when I needed it most. Mark Weisman has proven himself to be far more than a good friend and superb architect; his brilliant sketches have complemented the text in a way that adds a whole new dimension to the book. There is no adequate way to thank Frank Deford for the manner in which he has supported this project from the beginning. He has influenced the structure and tone of this book as much as anyone, and it is a special honor to have his fine writing gracing its opening pages. It was Frank who introduced me to Mike Towle, a competent and sensitive editor with whom it has been a delight to work. I am most grateful for Mike's referral of my manuscript to Ron Pitkin of Cumberland House. In Ron I have found a publisher who could not be a more perfect match; he has been captivated by the spirit of this book from the beginning, shown great respect for my wishes, and been more than generous with his time. In Ron and Mike, I have made two new friends in the process.

Finally, Christopher and I owe a huge debt of gratitude to his three siblings Matthew, Claire, and William for making these conversations possible. Their sensitivity to his need throughout one remarkable summer may have left them seemingly absent from large portions of the text that follows, but in truth they were never far away. They allowed us several uninterrupted segments of time to talk, and for that gift we thank them.

Out of life comes death,
and out of death, life.
Out of the young, the old,
and out of the old, the young.
Out of waking, sleep,
and out of sleep, waking.
The stream of creation and dissolution
never stops.

—Heraclitus[1]

INTRODUCTION

O ut of a sound sleep I sat straight up in bed. My first thought was that an odd noise must have awakened me, but the room was silent. By the dim light of the outdoor floodlights around the dormitory, I could see my roommate Alan sound asleep in his bed across the room. He was lying on his back with his mouth wide open, snoring ever so slightly. I turned my gaze to the right, where I could see my alarm clock softly glowing, its oversized numbers reading 2:37 A.M. Beyond the clock on my desk lay a neat stack of textbooks and notebooks ready for my next day's classes. Looking outside the large picture window that spanned the adjoining wall, I watched big snowflakes silently cascading down, laying a soft white carpet over the inner courtyard of our dormitory cluster; it had not been snowing when I went to bed. In the upper left corner of the window was our "McGovern for President" sticker from the previous fall. My gaze returned to Alan. Mystified as to the reason for my sudden awakening, I decided to lie down and go back to sleep. With that simple decision came the greatest single quantum shift in my perception of reality, a revelation the memory of which would stay fresh in my mind for the rest of my years, inescapably influencing the course of my life from that point onward.

It was February of 1973; I was nineteen years old, a freshman at Dartmouth College on the cold western border of New Hampshire. I did not consider myself a particularly religious person, having grown up saturated with more than enough "church" as the stepson of an Episcopal priest; I did not yet appreciate the difference between religion and spirituality. My interests had always rested solidly within the objective sciences and mathematics. The summer between my junior and senior years of high school was spent in Bar Harbor, Maine, conducting my own research project at the Jackson Laboratory, one of the finest mammalian genetics laboratories in the country, and I had entered Dartmouth with the explicit intent of becoming a physician-astronaut specializing in space medicine. I corresponded with astronaut Frank Borman, a gracious man and early role model who first captured my imagination when he read the creation story from the first chapter of Genesis while orbiting the moon on Christmas Eve in 1968. He generously shared with me his advice and encouragement, proposing that my best strategy for participating in the space program was to someday become a physician who would care for the crew of a future Mars mission during the long flight, and then function as a research biologist after we arrived on the surface of Mars. Given my overwhelming respect for Borman, I instantly adopted that as my life's goal.

At that time in my life, there was simply no room in my cranial space for realities other than those that could be scientifically proven through the application of objective, empirical methodology. If anyone had told me that my solidly grounded and carefully balanced worldview could be shaken apart within the space of five short minutes, I would have dismissed the suggestion as preposterous. Yet, as I sat on my bed at 2:37 A.M. on that cold and snowy February night in New Hampshire, that is precisely what was about to take place.

I wanted to lie down and go back to sleep, but soon found that I could not. At first the sensation was a relatively normal one of slipping off the bed. I had been sleeping too close to the side of the mattress, I thought, and my turning around to see the alarm clock had shifted my center of gravity just enough to send me over the edge. I instinctively extended my right arm to block my fall, but my hand passed right through the bed, and I kept falling. Only I really wasn't falling at all. If I had been, I would have already hit the floor by now. As bizarre as it might sound, I was *pouring*; slowly, but inexorably *pouring*, like molasses, off the edge of the bed and down toward the floor. I leaned as far as I could to the left, toward the bed, but it made no difference. My descent continued, and now, as I looked to the left, the top of the bed was at eye level. That was when I hit the floor. Actually, *hit* is probably the wrong word. There was no discernible impact but rather a soft termination to the descent, followed by a rebound. I was actually going back up again; I was *bouncing*. After another drop, I bounced again, this time looking at my sleeping roommate and straining to shout his name, to wake him up so that he could witness this extraordinary event in which I was defying the laws of physics in my own dormitory room, slowly bouncing around on the floor like a big balloon. But I could not shout; I could not speak a word. Still slowly bouncing, my anxiety rose at my inability to speak.

Is this a dream? I wondered, but it was so vivid and real; more real, in fact, than normal waking experience, and completely *unlike* a dream in its acute clarity. As I pondered the nature of this remarkable experience, I turned my gaze for the first time back toward my bed just as I came to

the top of a bounce. I was absolutely unpre-
pared for the sight that lay before me, for there I
saw *myself* lying in my bed, sound asleep. In that
moment I knew for the first time and forever that
my body and I were two different things.

The truly surprising thing about that moment
was the manner in which I accepted the whole
experience. Instead of reacting with total and
absolute terror at being dislocated from the one
and only piece of matter that I had ever identi-
fied as *myself*, it was rather as if I were remembering something that I had known a long, long
time ago and then forgotten at some indetermi-
nate point. I suddenly felt a freedom and exhila-
ration of a sort that was completely new to me,
yet part of a fuller and more natural form of existence than I had ever experienced back in that
slumbering shell of a body laid out on the bed.

A toilet flushed in the men's bathroom across
the hall outside our room. In the very moment of
my curiosity as to who might still be up, I found
myself moving toward the door to the hallway. I
sped up as I approached the door, and I
expected to bounce off the door as I had on the
floor, but in the next instant I was through the
door and awash in the stark synthetic glow of
the fluorescent ceiling lights that lit the corridors
at all hours of the day and night.

Another noise came from the bathroom. Facing the bathroom door, I passed right through it and found myself inside with Leonard, an upperclassman who lived in the only single room on the floor because of his habit of staying up most of the night studying. I watched him pick at his face in the mirror for a while, then, bored, I passed just as easily back out into the hallway. I was contemplating a jaunt outside around the campus in the snowstorm when I heard a door close directly overhead. I looked straight up, and immediately rose toward the ceiling. In the next moment I was through the ceiling, emerging into the second-floor hall. The door to the women's bathroom was in front of me, and one of the women was just going in, wearing a pink bathrobe in preparation for a shower. The thrill of my young lifetime lay just on the other side of that door.

Or so I had hoped. Much to my dismay, the more I focused my attention on that bathroom door, the more I felt a force pulling me away. I focused more intently on the door, and like a fully expanded rubber band, something tugged at me with an irresistible strength. In a single moment of time, I felt a *snap*, with an almost audible *pop!* and immediately I sat straight up in my bed, back in my room. I shot a quick glance at the alarm clock to my right; it read 2:42 A.M. Outside the picture window the large snowflakes were cascading silently down just as I had seen them before. I looked over at Alan. He was sleeping on his back, exactly as I had seen him, his mouth wide open and emitting the same soft snore. Jumping out of bed, I looked back this time at an empty set of sheets. I then heard the bathroom door close out in the hall. I ran to my door, opened it, and looked down the hall, where Leonard had just reached his room, a towel around his neck.

This was all just a little too much to have been a random dream, but one more test remained. The noise of a shower turned off upstairs. Waiting in the hallway for two or three minutes, I finally heard the dull thud of the upstairs bathroom door closing. Wearing only the underpants I had been sleeping in, I sprinted down the hall to the stairway, ran up to the second floor, and threw open the fire door to that hallway. A young woman was walking down the hallway in a pink bathrobe, the very same girl I had seen just minutes earlier, her wet hair now wrapped turban style in a towel. She shot a stunned look at me and I retreated, embarrassed, back down to the first floor. I ran out of the front door into the snowstorm and stood in the center of the courtyard, letting the snowflakes fall on my upturned face and chest. My mind was reeling, trying to sort out the implications of what had just happened, and yet I knew with an absolute certainty that my life would never again be the same.

My conscious and intentional spiritual journey began that February night in 1973, a quest for the elusive, intangible, and ineffable force referred to as "spirit" that I suddenly knew to be as real and true as any objectively verifiable phenomenon that I had studied through the scientific method. My journey subsequently led me through Eastern forms of meditation and to the feet of Maharishi Mahesh Yogi, with whom I studied in Europe for several months. Paradoxically, it was time spent with this diminutive Hindu monk, steeping myself in deep meditation and the wisdom of the East, that drew me mysteriously yet inescapably back to the Christian tradition that I had earlier dismissed as irrelevant. Eventually, I abandoned thoughts of medical school, and, after graduating from Dartmouth, I attended the divinity school at Yale University. I was then ordained a priest in the Episcopal Church, compelled in the end to explore inner space rather than outer space.

Not that the two modes of enquiry are mutually exclusive. Quite the contrary; as my inner life has deepened over the years, so has my interest in recent advances within the scientific community. In fact the two seem linked, qualitatively different paths leading toward the one common goal of understanding the Ultimate Mystery. In the spiritual path that Mystery is referred to as God; the Soul of the Universe; the Ground of all Being. In small particle theoretical physics, it is the Unified Field.

More and more, theoretical physicists are becoming aware that they are contemplating spiritual truths. They have refined both their technology and theory to the point that they now find themselves hovering on the very convergence of matter and spirit. Matter at its most basic level is observed to consist of pulses of energy lasting one ten-thousandth of a second, only to be continually replaced by consistently similar pulses. So the physicist is faced with an inherently spiritual question: What is the source of these pulses of energy that make up the entire material world in which we live and move and have our being? It is an *infinite* source, since the pulses continue indefinitely (matter does not just disappear), and it is an *intelligent* source, since the pulses keep replacing themselves with exactly the same type of pulses (material objects do not spontaneously change their size, shape, color, or texture without external manipulation). What could possibly be an in nite source of both energy and intelligence? Physicists have labeled it the Unified Field. Religions refer to it as God. A long-time friend and former room-mate of mine from college, who received his Ph.D. in physics from Harvard and now heads the physics department of a midwestern university, called me a few years ago to share what he thought was an irony. He and his colleagues were perusing the pages of Thomas Aquinas' *Summa Theologica* in an attempt to glean some insight as to where to head next with their research. He found it almost embarrassing to acknowledge, while I received the news with the most profound sense of rightness about the whole matter.

After my out-of-body experience in 1973, intriguing and revealing as it was, I found that it only raised another, greater question for me: Does the spirit endure? Does it endure after the death of the body? Despite my years of semi-nary studies, scouring the works of theologians on the subject, certain knowledge of the contin-uation of the soul after death ultimately came to me through my maternal grandmother.

Rowena Woodward, my grandmother, was a very significant figure in my early life. My natural father died when I was less than two years old, and my grandmother played a large role in bringing me up. The bond between us was as great as that between a mother and son, and we were best friends to boot. Never was that bond more pronounced to me than it was one day in the early eighties when I found myself involuntarily drawn into the middle of another inexplicable, supernatural event.

It was Palm Sunday 1982, and I was serving in my first parish, Christ Church Grosse Pointe, just north of Detroit. I was in good health, had no fever, and was taking no medications. Moreover, I was totally focused on the complex liturgy for the day in church—my grandmother was one of the last things on my mind. Now eighty-eight, she was in a convalescent facility back in my hometown of Bar Harbor, Maine. The senior minister with whom I worked was in the middle of celebrating our third Eucharist of the morning when, as I knelt beside the altar, I checked my watch; it was ten minutes before noon. The service, which had started at eleven o'clock, was right on time. With a sense of satisfaction, I closed my eyes and returned to my devotions with no clue of what was about to happen.

The acolytes thought I was about to faint, as I slumped forward a little and reached out my hand to steady myself against the altar. I would later learn that no one from the congregation had noticed anything unusual; but I had, for suddenly, there in the midst of a crowded Palm Sunday service, I was *with* my grandmother. Or she was with me. *In* me, in fact. Her presence was as real as if she had physically been there. It was *more* than real, as hard as that is to explain. I could feel her. I could smell her. And she was laughing; laughing with the same wild abandon and pure glee as she had so many years before when she and I ran headlong across a Maine pasture trying to fly a kite, only for both of us to slip on some cow manure instead. We sat there together in the soft grass smelling the pungent manure that now covered our shoes as we watched our beautiful kite sink into the waiting arms of the tallest elm tree bounding the pasture. We were both laughing so hysterically that we could not stand up, no matter how hard we tried. Only this time the laughter was more intense and her presence more vivid. It was the laughter of perfect and final freedom, and a presence of perfect and unconditional love, so much love that I could not bear it all, and I had to reach out to the side of the altar to keep from falling. And above it all and through the laughter, she spoke to me: "I'm fine. Everything is just fine—you'll see." That's all. It was over as quickly as it happened. In a moment of time I had witnessed my grandmother's resurrection, through which I have been given a lifetime of comfort and wisdom. Spirit does in fact endure.

I arrived home that Sunday at about one, and the telephone was ringing as I walked in. "I've got some bad news, Jeff," my mother said tearfully. "Gram had a stroke during the night, and she died just a little before noon this morning."

"I know," I found myself saying. "She stopped by to see me before she left."

"What?" came my mother's confused reply.

"Never mind," I said. "I'll explain when I see you."

It is only since 1982 that Easter has been for me a true celebration of Resurrection. Jesus' Resurrection. My grandmother's Resurrection. All of our Resurrections. I know for a fact that somehow, my grandmother was allowed to bring me that overwhelming good news as she passed over and on into the kingdom of life and love and laughter. She's fine. Everything is fine. I've only been allowed a mere glimpse, and that was overwhelming. Someday I will see it in all its outrageous fullness. We all will. And we will laugh. I know we will, because my grandmother laughed as she went in.

I have had many such experiences over the years, and I have seen angels. I have seen guardian angels standing watch over their charges, somber and intense in their purposefulness and quiet strength. I have seen angels of healing, totally focused on channeling energy toward a sick person in a hospital bed or an ambulance. There have been whole gatherings in ecstatic celestial dance above the altar of my church on Sunday mornings, seemingly drunk with joy and brushing up against one another like playful puppies. Moreover, it has long been my clear observation that the force of life pervades everything in nature. The sky swirls with streaming, darting, pulsating forms—the very ocean of air around us is constantly teeming with life. Every tree, bush, and plant shimmers with a corona of energy that flares out from its foliage, and every human being wears a garment of pure energy, beautiful beyond words, extending out at least a foot or more in all directions. The direct experience of these phenomena has lifted me from simple belief in the spiritual world—a sincere faith and hope in the eternal quality of life—to a level of certain knowledge, beyond any shadow of doubt. But that, to me, is the very cornerstone of the Christian faith: On the other side of any kind of death is always newer, greater life. Life never ends; it just keeps changing and growing. To *know*, deep within your heart and mind, that death is not an abrupt ending but rather a transition to more and more life, makes an extraordinary difference in the way you live. It brings a peace and joy and contentment to life that cannot be achieved in any other way.

I have needed that kind of comfort and peace, as my life has been punctuated by encounters with many kinds of death. The loss of my father before I was even two years old prompted continual speculation on my part throughout my childhood as to where he had gone, what he was doing, and whether I would ever see him again. My career as a parish priest has constantly thrown me into the midst of families wrestling with failure, loss, terminal illness, physical death, and all manner of conditions that the Jewish tradition regards as "living death," considered to be worse fates by far than simple physical death. Twenty years of counseling troubled parishioners has revealed to me the extent to which the fear of death—the terrifying sense that with the death of the body comes a complete and final cessation of all that we are—significantly prevents so many people from living a full and joyous life. I have personally lived through the horrible trauma of divorce, the worst form of death I have ever experienced. In each and every case, whether in my own life or in the lives of those I have served, I have observed a consistent pattern of new life springing from the ashes of death in any of its forms; life always prevails in the end. Always.

I do not want my children to feel trapped in an inexorable, one-way slide toward the graveyard, calling into question the ultimate meaningfulness of anything they do while they walk this earth. I want each of my four children to live with the liberating confidence of knowing that their present lives are part of a much greater, eternal existence, the full extent of which we can only begin to imagine from our present perspective. I believe that this is the greatest gift I can offer them as their father; it is only freedom from fear that allows us to live fully—risking, learning, growing, and loving to the fullest extent our human frames will allow.

This book is about such life. More particularly, it is about my nine-year-old son's intensive effort to reason his way out of a full-scale crisis over his own mortality by asking questions about every possible topic related to death. I agreed to discuss the subject with him, but only if we could talk about life instead, since death is truly a necessary part of the ongoing cycle of life. So it is quite accurate to say that this is a book about life. It is about the transition from one mode of life to another that forms the continuous pattern of our journeying through this wonderful, mystifying, paradoxical existence; an existence in which we all find ourselves midstream, unable to remember the location from which we arrived and unsure about our eventual destination.

The conversation contained in the following pages is, if we are willing to open ourselves to it, the dialogue that can occur between the adult and child within each one of us as we gradually find our way to spiritual maturity and take possession of that pearl of great price, within which lies our ultimate and eternal freedom.

Christopher's Summer

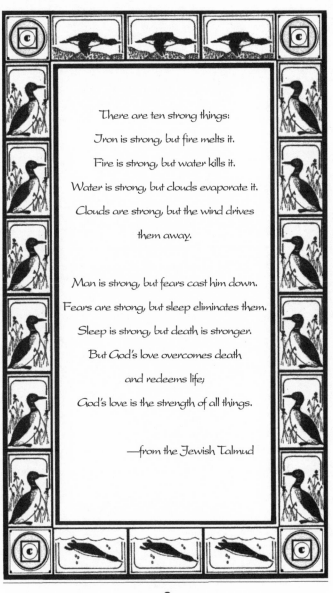

There are ten strong things:

Iron is strong, but fire melts it.

Fire is strong, but water kills it.

Water is strong, but clouds evaporate it.

Clouds are strong, but the wind drives

them away.

Man is strong, but fears cast him down.

Fears are strong, but sleep eliminates them.

Sleep is strong, but death is stronger.

But God's love overcomes death

and redeems life;

God's love is the strength of all things.

—from the Jewish Talmud

ONE

There is an island on a lake in Maine to which my family has returned faithfully every summer for thirty-eight years. It has been, for me, sacred space, a place for nurturing and shaping, a place for renewal. It functions in the same way for my four children, each of whom works diligently through the school year, yearning for the day when we will return together for another summer of living out our fondest dreams under the warm sun, blue sky, soft white pillow-like clouds, and the brilliant nighttime canopy of stars that do not cast down their healing light in just the same way anywhere else on this earth.

If you have seen the movie *On Golden Pond*, you have experienced something of the essence of our lake. Many dozens of similar lakes are dotted throughout northern New England, but this is the one that we have come to know, and its unique character and charm have become as essential to our being as the air we breathe and the food we eat. In the safety of its bounds we have been sustained through good times and bad. Here we have garnered the inner strength to weather storms of sorrow, failure, and loss.

And here, too, we have lifted our voices and our hearts together to sing and laugh and rejoice at the blessings bestowed upon us through the years.

Without television or video games, we rediscover just how much has been packed into this corner of creation, both to entertain and to teach. There are the quiet early morning hours, when mist shrouds pockets of the lake, and fishing is at its best; the hushed conversations that take place at these mystical times convey secrets of the heart that are shared gold, lasting a lifetime. The fat bass whose stomachs are full of newly swallowed crayfish, yet who still succumb to the endless variety of lures that ride our fishing lines, taste so fresh and sweet for breakfast, and give us some partial appreciation of what life was like for our ancestors, those who used to have to fish and hunt and forage every day for their food.

Children too young to engage in serious fishing delight in outwitting sunfish and minnow alike by holding a net very still off the side of the dock, and hoisting their hapless victims to the surface when curiosity draws them too close. The net is emptied into a large bucket of water until there are too many fish for the bucket, at which time they are poured back into the lake, and the contest begins all over again. Hunting for salamanders under rotted logs in the woods is fun, and endless hours can be spent flushing crayfish out from under rocks in the shallow reaches of the shore or snorkeling for freshwater mussels. Painted turtles that venture too close to the dock sometimes find themselves caught, too. The large snapping turtles that ply their way through the waters, however, enjoy complete immunity from capture; barring the occasional tentative jab from an oar held by a distant arm, they are far too dangerous for us to risk the bite that they can inflict if threatened. Respect for all "life-forms," as my son Christopher refers to them, is nurtured from an early age here. Apart from the bass and white perch that grace our table from time to time, all creatures taken captive during the day are released before sunset so that they may find their way back to their respective homes by nightfall. Best of all are the clear evenings, those legendary Maine summer evenings when the dry, cool air settles in, the water shimmers with the light of the moon, and the stars' light pierces through the black night sky with a brilliance that amazes you each time you see it.

While shepherding a group of my parishioners through the Holy Land a few years ago, I was told by one of our guides of an experience he once had in the Sinai desert. Stranded by a broken vehicle, he was forced to spend a night in the desert with some Bedouin shepherds. Strolling away from the campfire to the top of a sand dune at about midnight, he suddenly had a view of the heavens that made him reel; it was, he told me, as if he had never seen the stars before, they were so brilliant. With nothing but sand stretching off into the distance in every direction, and with no earthly light pollution interfering with the light of the stars, the resulting field of vision contained nothing but stars— the brightest, most vivid canopy of stars he had ever seen.

That account comes closest to describing the feeling that we have every time we anchor our boat in the middle of the lake, lie down on our backs, and observe the night sky. It is the perfect ending to a day in Maine: after a supper of lobsters, clams, and sweet Maine corn, with wild blueberry shortcake for dessert, after all children have washed off the dirt of the day and put on their pajamas, we get into the boat, drive to the center of the lake, drop anchor, and watch the sky. It is an awesome, sometimes overwhelming experience. Just a few years ago, Matthew, my eldest, jumped up with a start after contemplating the sky for a while and announced that he had to go back home right away. He was scared. When the night sky encompasses your entire field of vision, it is as if you are an astronaut floating in space, observing the universe that stretches out before you. You begin to try to gauge distances in what you are seeing. Once in a while a satellite flies by—a dim, solid white speck that arcs through the sky pretty quickly compared to an airplane; those, you know, are fairly close. The moon is a little farther away but still close. You then begin to pick out the planets that are visible; they are brighter than the surrounding stars, and they don't "twinkle" the way that stars do. They, and you, are all orbiting the same sun.

Eventually you make out the long, cloudy, white belt that stretches part way across the sky; this is the other end of the Milky Way, the galaxy in which our solar system resides—this is "home," even though the milky "cloud" we see contains millions of stars and solar systems similar to our own, at distances from us that boggle the mind. It was the next step in the cosmic tour I was giving my children one night that understandably set Matthew's head reeling. I was directing their gaze out beyond "home," out beyond the vast immensity of our own galaxy, to the spaces that lie still farther out. I was explaining that most of the "stars" that we see twinkling in our sky at night are not, in fact, stars at all, but whole galaxies, each comprised of millions and even billions of stars and solar systems. Suddenly, Matthew inadvertently reversed the viewing angle: He started imagining himself from the perspective of the farthest galaxies, and in short order experienced himself diminishing in size to the tiniest grain of sand, floating in the vastness of interstellar space, an insignificant piece of dust in an infinite tumble of planets and stars and galaxies and . . . it was just too much for his mind to handle. I have had that same experience several times. It is inevitable if you are going to throw your mind's eye out over such distances. At some point, your mind is going to look back upon itself, and you will, in that moment, at once see the enormity of the universe and the insignificantly tiny role you play in it all. It is both sobering and terrifying—a good healthy dose of "reality therapy" for the soul.

But to turn and run at the point of terror is to miss the next and grandest step in the celestial tour; for just where we seem to be on the brink of disappearing altogether in the face of the vastness that lies all around us, just one tiny step beyond the terrifying realization of how truly small and vulnerable we are in the larger scheme of things, just at that point lies new ground on which we can regain our balance and rebuild our confidence. Just beyond that boundary of spine-tingling terror lies God. Not some white-haired, bearded old man who casts his benevolent eye toward us from the sky, an anthropomorphic deity whom we have created in our own image, but something far greater, far more mysterious, far more inspiring, far more comforting, and far more real. For there, just at the boundary between here and infinity, just where our little knowledge turns into fear and our proud psyches have the celestial rug pulled out from under them and begin the bone-chilling free fall into the black vortex of insignificance, just there is the very point at which "the Light shines in the darkness" as Saint John so clearly observed. There, we realize that no matter how small we seem, no matter how dark it may get, the darkness has not overcome the Light, and never will.

The loving force that created us and all other "life-forms" is in the very fiber of this cold, apparently lifeless universe. Not male, not female, not human, not alien; totally incomprehensible in nature, the Spirit of God fills the entire cosmic space and all of time, and dwells beyond it all as well. Creator and prime mover of all that is, God also created us and cares for us, endowing our tiny insignificance with eternal and ultimate value. Why? We do not know. We only know that it was God's great pleasure to do so, and that we are thereby graced with an unimaginably valuable gift—a share of God's own life-force pulsing within us, and this beautiful planet on which to enjoy it. Our presumption that ownership and control of the miraculous gift of life is our own ultimately leads us into paralyzing fears, fears that grow out of the illusion that we are gazing out at this large and intimidating universe naked, as it were; that we are marooned here entirely and utterly on our own.

It is this lake, the ever-dancing waters and the fish beneath them, the loons that paddle its surface and entertain us nightly with their haunting cries, the great blue herons that stand motionless on their high perches and then swoop down to grab unsuspecting fish from just below the surface, the stately old pines and lichen-covered rocks that stand sentinel upon its shores; it is this lake, with the great cycle of life that continuously surrounds it and throbs within it, and especially the canopy of stars that covers it at

night like a shimmering blanket; it is this lake that has taught me so much about life and death and everything in between, and has led me, in the course of my earthly pilgrimage thus far, to an ever-greater appreciation of the inevitability, vastness, and transcendent mystery of God. And it was in this sacred spot that my son Christopher approached me concerning the most elusive and intimidating subject there probably is for any of us: the very nature and meaning of death.

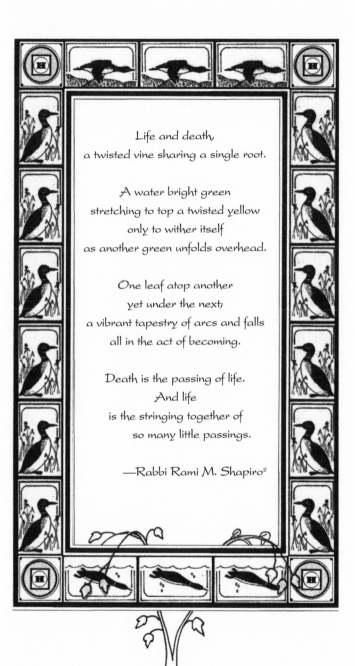

Life and death,
a twisted vine sharing a single root.

A water bright green
stretching to top a twisted yellow
only to wither itself
as another green unfolds overhead.

One leaf atop another
yet under the next;
a vibrant tapestry of arcs and falls
all in the act of becoming.

Death is the passing of life.
And life
is the stringing together of
so many little passings.

—Rabbi Rami M. Shapiro[2]

TWO

My nine-year-old son was in crisis. It wasn't planned, and he certainly didn't welcome it. This particular crisis doesn't normally occur until a much later age and never strikes some people at all. But Christopher is a serious, pensive sort of child. He wants to understand every single detail of the world in which he lives and his part within it. He has always been that way. From the moment he emerged into this world, he has had a level of intelligence and probing curiosity that have driven him to inquire deeply into the workings of everything he sees around him, and to question all of the assumptions that the rest of us usually take for granted. It is at once his greatest blessing and curse. While he was still an infant, his only goal in life was to sit up. Once he could sit, he worked intently toward the single goal of standing. Not content to be able to stand on his own at the tender age of five-and-a-half months, he spent every waking moment attempting to walk, a skill which he acquired early in his seventh month—earlier by far than his mother and I were prepared for, and shortly before he began to display an obvious affinity for classical music.

So it really shouldn't have come as any great surprise to me when, at a mere nine years of age, Christopher suddenly became acutely aware of his own mortality. We were sitting in the hammock together in our bathing suits, sucking on Popsicles and looking out over the lake at loons passing close by on a perfect, sunny June day in Maine. There was a gentle cool breeze coming in from the lake, its fresh smell mingling with the slightest scent of spruce and pine. Tucked nearby in the lowest, moist ground of the woods, the pink and white of rare lady's-slippers were in the midst of their all-too-brief flowering, and the yellow-streaked purple wild iris had just burst forth, claiming dominance over the water's edge. Christopher's sister and two brothers were horsing around in the water by the beach, each one trying to imitate the scariest water monsters they could dream up. Everything around us was radiant and singing with life, when the dark, intimidating shadow forced its way up from the depths of his nine-year-old mind and broke to the surface:

"I'm going to die."

18

"What?"

"I'm going to die. But when? When do you think I'm going to die?"

"Why Christopher, that's not something you have to think about at your age. You have your whole life ahead of you, years and years of having fun and growing and learning . . ."

"But then I'm going to die. So are you. I need to know when and how. I don't want it to be painful. What is it like when you die? What is it like, and where do we go? You're a minister, so you know about these things. You have to tell me. God promises us in the Bible that we'll go to heaven, but how do we know that is true? It's just a book. What if there really isn't a heaven— what if it's all a lie? What if we die and that's the end—what if there's nothing more at all? And then what's the point of anything that I do here?"

I was suddenly the father of a child obsessed with the nature of death and the purpose of life. He had applied himself to understanding nearly everything else in his world—why not the nature of life and death? Attempts to placate or divert his attention did nothing but make his determination more intense. Morning, noon, and night, his only desire was to talk about death. So strongly resolved was his mind to solve this ultimate enigma, it turned out that he had brought the subject up casually with everyone with whom he had come into contact over the past month: his teacher, the school counselor, his mother, his friends, strangers . . . and now with some urgency, me. "You're a minister, so you know about these things. Tell me." My son was crying out for help, and I recognized in his inquiry the very same questions that I had asked when I had been his age.

So it was, in my forty-fourth year of participation in this grand mystery of human life, that my son and I set out together to examine the twin phenomena of life and death. And when I say together, I mean that it was truly a joint effort. Death was certainly a subject that I had dealt with many times during twenty years of parish ministry. In sermons, Sunday School, adult education classes, and individual counseling sessions, I had become well-versed in quoting just the right Bible passages, summarizing the Church's best theologians, and generally affirming and intellectualizing the bedrock Christian belief that life does not end with physical death but changes and continues in ways that we cannot presently understand. But this was my son, a part of me. And in his questions were distantly familiar and unsettling chords that resonated deep within me, echoing similar questions posed years ago by another little boy who was "much too young to be thinking about such things." I realized at the outset that my dialogue with Christopher was also to be a dialogue with that other little boy from so long ago, whose questions were never answered directly or adequately, but rather brushed aside by well-meaning adults who were part of a generation that never talked about death. It had been too morbid a subject to discuss in depth, or for too long by persons who were happy and healthy and fully engaged in life.

It had taken me nearly thirty years to come to terms with my early questions about death, and my years of theological training and ordination may have been a subconscious but integral part of that quest. I must admit, though, that the years I spent in formal theological training left me ill-prepared to deal directly and openly with questions and fears regarding death. I was equipped only to hold my own intellectually in affirming the Church's traditional teaching and theology on the matter. Such complex intellectual constructs may well be important cornerstones in the formal body of Christian theological teaching as it has been articulated and developed over the centuries, but it does little or nothing for a frightened little nine-year-old asking his father for help in overcoming the paralyzing fear and foreboding that everything we value most in life comes to an abrupt and empty termination with death. The only adequate responses for a frightened nine-year-old (or ninety-nine-year-old) are the responses that come from the heart; person-to-person, soul-to-soul.

Ironically, the fearful little boy within me only received true comfort from those who are dying. It has been my privilege over the past couple of decades to be associated with the Hospice movement, ministering to those who are terminally ill and have six months or less to live. It is probably more accurate to say that I have been *ministered to* by many people in their final days and hours of life. I have learned more about the meaning of life and death from people who are dying than from any other source.

But how was I to make sense of it all to this young boy, this Christopher, who was searching, as I had for so long, for the comfort and solace of true, grounded faith? Was there any way to give him that gift at an earlier age and with less struggle than I had experienced? How could I best distill more than thirty years of education, seeking and finding into language and images to which Christopher could relate—language and images that would truly address and answer his questions, and not merely put him off until another day? Christopher had to be a full participant in this endeavor, not simply a passive listener. I needed his input; I needed to know which images made sense to him and which ones did not. Christopher needed to guide me through this quest. And I knew my son well enough to sense that the intensity of his interest had him well-primed for the endeavor. I had no idea in that moment just how primed he really was, although I did know that he was expecting an awful lot from me: "You're a minister, so you know about these things. Tell me." I sent up a silent prayer, and I couldn't help but smile as that old adage went through my mind: "They say that God never gives us any more than we can handle; I just wish he didn't have quite so much confidence in me."

You would know the secret of death.

But how shall you find it unless you

seek it in the heart of life?

. . . If you would indeed behold the

spirit of death, open your heart wide

unto the body of life.

For life and death are one, even as

the river and the sea are one.

—Kahlil Gibran[3]

THREE

"So when do we start the first lesson, Dad?" Christopher asked, looking at me with a serious and expectant face from across the hammock. Two young chipmunks jabbered at each other directly over our heads as a contested nut came hurtling down to the forest floor.

"Lessons?" I replied.

"Yes. Lessons on death. You are always teaching classes at church about the Bible and history and stuff like that, so I just figured that you would probably want to teach me about death in the same way—different lessons, like you do at church."

"How many lessons do you think this will take?" I asked with some trepidation.

"Well, it's a big subject, and it really scares me a lot, so I figure that it will take quite a few until I'm not scared by it anymore."

"And when do you think that we'll have time for all these lessons?" I asked. "Our days are pretty busy with swimming, water-skiing, tubing, and everything else that you and your brothers and sister like to do each day. It's not fair for me to spend a lot of time with you and not with them."

"I've thought of that," Christopher said, "and I think that the best time for our lessons on death would be at reading time each day, because the other kids will be busy then, and it will be quiet."

"No," I said. "You have books that you have to read for school this summer, and you are not going to get out of it by talking to me instead."

A little smile broke over his face just then. I wasn't sure if it was because I had seen through his ploy to escape from his summer reading or if his suggestion was sincere, and he honestly hadn't seen the escape potential in it all until now. Whichever was the case, Christopher, my consummate negotiator, didn't miss a beat.

"How about at bedtime?" he suggested.

"Nope. We're not going to discuss death just before you go to bed, because it is the very thought of it that has been keeping you awake at night," I said.

"Then we could do it at different times, when-ever we have a few minutes alone," he sug-gested. "It could be in the morning one day, if everyone else is in the water, or we could even talk on the way to the grocery store (the nearest grocery store is about a half-hour's drive from our lake). Can we do it that way?"

"Okay. I'm comfortable with that," I said. "But let's change one thing. Instead of calling these lessons about death, I would rather think of them as lessons about life. Is that all right with you?"

"Not really," Christopher stated. "I want to know about death."

"But what if I can show you that death is really a part of life?" I asked him.

"That would be okay with me—as long as we are talking about death," he said.

"It's a deal," I replied. "We'll talk about how death is a part of life."

"Deal," Christopher said. "So when do I have my first lesson?"

"Well, when do you think the best time would be?"

"How about right now?" he quickly volunteered.

I winced inside; I was half expecting that reply. I had so hoped that I could have at least a day to organize my thoughts and come up with a plan of attack. But this subject had been on Christopher's mind for a few weeks now, and I knew how anxious he was to talk about it. I couldn't put him off any longer. I would just have to put him to work right from the beginning as a full participant in these conversations. I quickly scoped the territory around us for the three other kids. Matthew was lying on the dock in the sun; Claire and William had loaded a piece of freshwater mussel into a net, and were now sitting absolutely still, waiting to catch unsuspecting sunfish.

"Okay," I said. "You're in luck. We'll have the first lesson. Where do you think that we should start?"

"I get to pick?"

"Yes; what do you want to talk about first?"

He immediately said, "Well, before we talk about anything else, I think that I would like to know what you think about NDEs."

"NDEs?" I asked, with what was probably a totally blank look on my face. Within the next five seconds, I could see the erosion of confidence in Christopher's face. Not a good start.

"Are you telling me that you don't even know what NDEs are?" Christopher asked wide-eyed. Feeling defensive, I felt that we needed to set down some rules before we ventured any further into this discussion.

"Christopher, there are a lot of things that I do not know, and I am going to be perfectly honest with you when that is the case. And I want you to do the same with me. Whenever you don't understand something I have said, tell me, and I will try to explain it in a better way. Remember: We said that we were going to do this together, so we have to help each other, okay?"

"Okay . . . sure. Would you like me to tell you what NDEs are?" I had the strange feeling that the teacher-student roles in this dialogue had suddenly switched.

"I think that would help me a lot," I answered appreciatively.

"Well, NDE stands for Near Death Experience, which is sometimes what happens when people die and then the doctor brings them back to life."

"Yes," I said, recovering. "I do know about NDEs. I just didn't know what the letters NDE stood for."

"There was this one woman in the hospital that I heard about, and she died, and the hospital called her house so that the baby-sitter could bring her daughter in to say good-bye to her, and the baby-sitter dressed the little girl in a hurry and got all her clothes mismatched. Well, before the daughter and the baby-sitter got to the hospital, the woman suddenly came back to life, and woke up, and do you know what the first thing she said was?"

"Boo!" I said, making Christopher jump and almost fall out of the hammock.

Composing himself, he said, "No, Dad; this is serious."

"I'm sorry, I just thought it would be funny if everyone thought that she was dead and she suddenly woke up and said, 'Boo.'"

"Well she didn't say that at all," Christopher corrected me, without a smile. "The first thing she said was, 'Why is my daughter dressed in such awful clothes today?' The nurses didn't know what she was talking about until a couple of minutes later, when the baby-sitter rushed in with her daughter, and they all saw that none of the clothes she had on matched at all. She even had on two different-colored socks. Isn't that awesome?"

"Awesome," I agreed.

"It's like she could see what her daughter was wearing, even though she was dead, and even though her daughter wasn't even in the room."

"Did you know that things like that happen a lot?" I said.

"They do?"

"They sure do; more than most people realize. It doesn't just happen when people die and come back; lots of people come back from being unconscious in a coma and say that they saw and heard everything that was going on around them while they were in the coma."

Christopher paused for a moment, looking out over the lake. "It's interesting that people do that when they are real sick, but I think it's way more interesting that a dead person could do that."

"Yes," I said, "I guess it is."

32

"So what do you think about NDEs?"

"What do I think about them?"

"Yes. Do you think that they are really proof that we don't actually die?"

"Christopher," I said, "I don't think that there is any solid proof of that, even though I absolutely believe that death is not an ending but simply a change, like a caterpillar transforming itself into a butterfly. But so many NDEs have been reported over the past few years that it lets us know that *something* is going on there, right?"

"Right. But what do you think it means?" he asked.

"Well, the important thing about NDEs for me," I said, "is that most everyone who has the experience seems to have the same experience. They have interviewed people from all over the world who have gone through this, and most of them say that when they died, they had the experience of going through something like a tunnel with a light at the other end. When they come out of the tunnel into the light, they are greeted by a whole bunch of people who turn out to be friends and family members who have already passed on. They are there to greet them, and to lead them toward a very bright light. Most people say that the place feels familiar; that they remember it, as if they have come home. When they get near the

33

bright light, there is a very radiant being of pure light who is standing in the way who says, 'It is not time for you to die yet; you need to go back.' And that is when they go back to their bodies and wake up. And they remember what happened for the rest of their lives here. Most of them have this same experience, no matter how old they are, or whether they are men or women, or what country they are from, or even what religion they belong to. That tells me that it must be real. If people were making it up, then everybody would have a different story, don't you think?"

"Yes," replied my son, a most analytical look on his face. "That's logical." A slight pause, and then, "Have you ever known someone who had an NDE?"

"Yes. I've known two."

"Did they have that same experience?"

"Yes. Exactly the same. And it was so real for them that they said that they could never be afraid of death again, ever."

"Did they tell you about the experience themselves, or did you just hear about it from somebody else?"

"They told me about it themselves," I assured him.

"Hmmm," he said, while he weighed the credibility of the evidence. And then, almost as an afterthought, "You never died and came back, because you're not old enough; right, Dad?"

"Actually, I did die and come back once, a long time ago." Christopher turned just then and looked at me, his eyes widening in disbelief. "It's not just older people who die and come back," I said. His eyes were fixed on me, his whole face a mixture of shock and anticipation.

"Dad," he implored me, a new urgency in his voice, "Why didn't you tell me about this?"

"About what?"

"About your NDE."

Why had I let the focus turn to me, right at this particular moment? His face was so full of hope and expectation at what I was about to say to him. His heart was soaring now, so sure that his father was about to reveal to him a firsthand account of the secrets of death, an account that he could trust in and believe, because it came from his dad.

"I didn't have a Near Death Experience, Christopher."

"But you just said . . . "

"I said that I died once for a short time, and then they brought me back. That's all that happened."

My mind raced back, as it had done a hundred times before, to the day it happened, scouring my memory for anything—anything I might have overlooked. How I wanted to give my son that gift—the comfort that I had so desperately wanted myself after it had happened. I was on the operating table in the hospital, a junior in high school with a chronic cough and a shadow in my right lung, and the doctor was preparing me for a bronchogram, a test in which they would squirt some radioactive liquid into my lung and watch it disperse with an X-ray machine. I kept coughing up the tube that was inserted through my mouth into my windpipe, so the doctor kept injecting more and more topical xylocaine, an anesthetic, directly into my lungs through a needle he had placed in my trachea. The needle hurt, I was scared, the doctor kept looking at his watch—frustrated that he was running so far behind, and yet I could not tolerate that tube that he was trying to push down my throat. Finally, the doctor said, "Let's stop playing games with this, okay?" and with that, he pushed about half a syringe more of xylocaine directly into my lungs. I felt the cold fluid flood down into my lungs, and noted with some fascination that I had no urge to cough at all. Then, in the next instant, I felt my back arch involuntarily up off the table, and my arms stiffen out straight on

36

both sides of me like wings. Wondering what was going on, I looked up into the eyes of my doctor, which even through his glasses and surgical mask were suddenly and clearly wide with fear, and I heard him say, "Oh, shit!" That was the last thing I remembered. I had tried so hard, so many times, to remember more, just a fleeting image or a dim glimpse of the tunnel, or the loved ones, or the light, or anything while I was gone. They said later that with that last massive dose of xylocaine my heart and breathing had all stopped for several minutes as the terrified doctor tried everything he knew to bring back this poor teenager who had fallen victim to a massive overdose administered by an impatient and, therefore, careless physician whose mind was already on his next patient. I was clinically dead for several minutes. I woke up in the recovery room later and turned my head to see an old man lying on the bed next to mine. Just at that moment a surge of blood came vomiting out of his mouth. The nurses came running over and whisked him out of the room. It seemed to me that I was in hell, not heaven, and I turned my head back and dozed for another couple of hours before they would let my parents take me home. But of those several minutes that I was clinically dead, seconds and minutes stretching out, one after the other—it must have seemed like an eternity to the doctor—of those several minutes I had not one memory, good nor bad. Heaven nor Hell. Nothing. And after all that, it turned out that the "shadow" on my right lung was the fault of the X-ray machine, my chronic cough an allergy to dust. I felt cheated—a victim of friendly fire. And I felt I was shortchanging Christopher now, as I related to him the briefest details of my temporary demise so long ago, and watched his gaze drop to the ground, his eyes clouded with disillusionment and disappointment.

"There may be lots of stories about NDEs," he said, "but if you died and it didn't happen to you, then I don't know if I can believe that it actually happens to other people. It's not logical. I'm going swimming." With that, the first lesson was over, and I was left alone in the hammock feeling a little unsure of where we would go next in these discussions.

A painted turtle popped its head out of the water not far from the beach, looked around for a minute or so, and disappeared under the water again. I thought about its long winter at the bottom of the lake, burrowed under the mud. Near freezing, no air to breathe, nothing to eat,

metabolism near zero. What does it experience during that long hibernation, so close to death—anything? And after those long months hovering near death, who wakes it up again, to rise to the surface and take its first breath of air in months, and bask in the sunlight? A sacred mystery. However he accomplished it, God certainly fashioned an extraordinary world.

Life is like the Bengal tiger,

marching through the jungle;

You can stand and fight him,

though you will surely die;

Or, you can jump on his back

and ride like the wind.

—Hindu saying

FOUR

Water is the usual domain of fish, not birds, but within it, loons are incredibly agile and quick—quicker, in fact, than the fish for which they hunt. Paddling along the surface of the lake in groups of two or three, each will intermittently thrust its whole head and neck into the water to look for fish. When some fish are located, the loon will immediately disappear, diving down to try to catch its next meal, resurfacing quite a distance from the point at which it disappeared. I have always marveled at the amount of distance they cover underwater in a relatively short period of time, but only once have I actually seen a loon swimming underwater.

My daughter Claire and I were out in the canoe one day, pausing as we came upon two loons floating along the surface in a shallow area of the lake. Without a sound, we slowly paddled closer and closer until we were only three feet from the closest loon. Watching us carefully with its brilliant red eyes, the bird finally reached the limit of its comfort zone, suddenly diving to put some distance between us underwater. As Claire and I were positioned between the loon and the rest of the lake, however, the loon had to swim directly under our canoe to reach open water. The sight was impressive to say the least: With its wings swept back along its sides, legs and webbed feet thrust straight behind itself, and head and neck straining out ahead, the bird knifed through the water at an incredible speed. We were able to observe it as it passed under our canoe, and in those few seconds it resembled a penguin in the way that it seemed to effortlessly negotiate its way underwater at remarkable speed.

Above the water it is a far different story. Loons are one of the most ungainly birds of all when it comes to making the transition from water to air. The first indication that a loon is going to try to take off comes with the sudden sound of slapping from out on the water. Loud slapping. Repetitive, loud slapping. If you are fortunate enough to be within eyesight of the bird, you will see its large wings completely extended, apparently just beating the water with them. After a few seconds, however, it begins to move forward, gradually gaining speed until its body rises bit-by-bit out of the water. Then, after fifteen or twenty seconds of such a gargantuan expenditure of energy, the bird's large webbed feet suddenly pop up out of the water in a dead run. The sound changes now, as the wings are simply flapping, and the bird's big, webbed feet begin their own style of slapping, generating a faster and more staccato sound on the water than the wings. For another fifty yards, the vision of this large black and white bird beating its wings and running over the surface of the water at the same time is comical, and you wonder if the poor thing is ever going to be able to take off. Often, after the huge expenditure of energy just to get its body out of the water, after slapping and flapping and running across half the lake, it simply stops dead, settles back down into the water and gives up for the moment, exhausted. But sometimes it makes it, clearing the water's surface and gracefully arcing up into the sky, beautiful and strong.

My first discussion with Christopher left me feeling that we had been like a couple of loons, slapping and flapping our way into it, trying to get it off the ground, and then having it all come to an abrupt end. I hoped then that the similarities would continue, and that after a little rest, we could both make another attempt. Oddly enough, the next conversation began in the car unexpectedly, a day or two later, as all four children and I were coming back from the store.

One of my kids' favorite activities is safe only on the little one-way road that goes around the island in Maine, because there is very little traffic there. They call it "sky riding." We open the sunroof in the car and they stand up on the front seat, their chests and heads sticking out above the roof, and I drive. They love the breeze on their faces and the feeling of importance as we pass a neighbor and they get to look down and say hello from up so high. On this particular day there was a healthy breeze coming in from the lake to begin with, and as we passed over the causeway and onto the island, I was driving directly into that breeze, which made it even stronger. The kids loved it and were laughing hysterically at what it was doing to their hair. Laughing, singing, and howling like wolves all the way around the island, they didn't want to stop once we reached our driveway, so I drove them around again.

"That was awesome!" Christopher yelled as he tumbled out of the car, his hair still standing straight up in front.

"Was it?" I replied.

"Oh, yeah—that wind, it makes you feel like you're flying!" he said.

"Well, if you liked *that*, just wait until I get you out on the boat!" I said, an idea suddenly forming in my mind.

"Why?" he asked.

"Because the wind is stronger out on the lake, before it hits all these trees, and I can go faster in the boat with you than I feel safe doing when you are standing up in the car, so instead of just standing up straight and looking funny, your hair might just blow right off your head!" I said.

"Then I'll look like you," he said, laughing and pointing to my shiny head. "Oh, no!"

The promise of an impending boat ride was all the incentive the kids needed to help unpack and put away groceries, and soon we were out on the lake, slicing straight into the wind at about forty-five miles per hour, making the apparent speed of the wind sixty or seventy miles per hour. William, who is only six, decided that he didn't like it at all, so he quickly retreated to his secret onboard shelter, an open storage area under the dashboard that he calls his "dressing room," away from the wind and spray. But the other three loved it, Christopher the most. He had positioned himself up in the very point of the bow, kneeling on the cushion there and holding the bow line in both hands as we raced through the choppy water. Above the din of the wind and waves and motor, I could just make out his voice:

"Dad!" he yelled, a smile seeming to stretch from ear to ear.

"*What?*" I yelled back.

"This is amazing!" he screamed back. "I can't even see the boat up here; I feel like I'm flying over the water like Superman! I feel so free!" I noticed that his hair, in fact, had not blown completely off his head, but rather was plastered straight back, instead of merely standing up straight as it had after sky riding in the car. And that smile—I hadn't seen a smile like that on his face for a long time.

"Remember that feeling!" I shouted back.

Later, after our return to the dock, I realized that it was time to walk the dog, and I asked Christopher to join me. As we began to make our way around the island, I intentionally said nothing. After a short while, Christopher broke the silence.

"Dad?"

"Yes?"

"In the boat, why did you tell me to remember that feeling?"

"Do you remember it?"

"Yes—it was awesome."

"Did it feel the same as when you were sky riding?"

"Yes, only ten times more."

"Ten times more *what*?"

Our footsteps formed a cadence in the gravel as we walked on, as Christopher reflected on my question.

"I don't know how to say it very well, Dad, except that when I am sky riding, or going fast in the boat, or when I was running in that pasture the other day, I feel different—free."

"Happy?"

"Oh, yeah."

"As if you could do anything?"

"Yeah—in the boat, it was just like I was flying. I could fly!"

"Christopher," I said, stopping and turning to him, "A couple of days ago, we had our first discussion about death, and you picked the topic, right?"

"Yes."

"Well," I went on, "I want to have another discussion with you now, and I want to pick the subject. Is that okay with you?"

49

"Sure," he said, and then, "but I don't know if I want to talk about death *now*—I mean, right after I've had so much fun, you know?"

"Uh-huh, but remember when I told you that I wanted these discussions to be about life, not death?"

"Oh, so you mean that you want to talk about life right now?"

"Yes."

"Okay."

Our greyhound, a former racer, had stood still long enough and was now pulling at her leash to continue on. We started moving again, which pleased her greatly.

"Christopher, I want to ask you a question, and I really want you to think before you answer, so you can give me the best answer possible."

His face suddenly got serious. He said, "Okay. What's the question?"

"Who are you?" I asked.

"What?" he said immediately.

"Who are you?" I asked again.

"Dad—what kind of question is that?" he replied, "and what does it have to do with death?"

"It's a very important question," I said, "and just a minute ago, you told me that you would give me the very best answer that you could."

"But Dad," he said, clear frustration in his voice, "it's not a logical question for you to ask me . . . I mean, you already know who I am!"

"Yes, I do know who you are, but do you?" I replied.

"Do . . . I . . . know . . . who . . . I . . . am?" he said, slowly, accentuating each word, to highlight the ridiculous nature of the question.

"Well, do you?"

"Dad—of *course* I know who I am. After all, *I'm* the one who's *me*," he said. His tone of voice was beginning to take on the same quality that it had when he couldn't believe I didn't know what NDEs were.

"Okay," I said. "Then tell me who you are."

"I'm Christopher," he said.

"That's a name that your mom and I gave you when you were born, but that's all it is. Who are you? Who is Christopher Dugan?"

"Well," he replied, trying another approach, "I'm nine years old, and I'm going into fourth grade this year, and I play the cello, and I live in . . ."

"Christopher," I interrupted him, "that is a list of all the things you *do*. But *who* is doing all those things? *Who* is growing older? *Who* is going to school? *Who* plays that cello? *Who* lives in your house?"

At that, my son stopped and stood absolutely still in the middle of the street, his eyes fixed on me, his whole face a beacon of incredulous disbelief—a "What's wrong with this picture?" or "My father is actually going insane right in front of me right now" kind of look. But still humoring me, or perhaps just wanting to gauge the extent to which I was still in touch with reality, he answered my question, with the very same face, and in a very soft voice "Me."

And in an even softer voice, almost a whisper, I said, "And who are you?"

With that, Christopher ran toward me, his hands waving back and forth in front of my face, while he jumped up and down and shouted, "I'm *me*, Dad! Me—Christopher! I'm the one who is doing all those things! Why do you keep asking me this?"

"Because," I said, grasping his shoulders in my hands, looking straight into his eyes, "you have told me that you are going to die some day, and that scares you. You are afraid that you're going to die. And I'm asking you if you know who you really are. *Who* is going to die, Christopher?"

"I am," he said, and then, looking down at himself, "My whole body."

"Is *that* you, then? Is your body all there is of you?"

Another "I cannot even believe he just said that" look, but no answer.

"What if I could prove to you that you are not just your body—that you are *more* than just your body?" I asked.

"How can you do that?" he said.

"Did you know that you have had two completely different bodies in your life so far?" I asked him.

"No, I haven't," he said. "I've only had one."

"Oh," I replied, "so you didn't even notice that it happened. Wow."

"Notice when *what* happened?"

"When you got your second body," I said.

"I *never* have gotten a second body," he insisted.

"But you *have*, Christopher. You've had your second one for about two years now. I've changed bodies about six times myself." That was when I received the "My father thinks he's a character from *Star Trek*" look.

"Dad, none of this is logical," he said, sounding, of course, like a certain popular *Star Trek* character.

"Oh, but it *is*," I replied. "You've learned about cells in school, haven't you?"

"Sort of," he said.

"You know that your whole body is made up of different kinds of cells, all working together, right?"

"Yes."

"Good. Like every other living thing, cells don't live forever. They die when they get old. And when they die, they are replaced by other cells that are new. Now, how long do you think it takes for every cell in your body to die and be replaced by completely new ones?" I asked.

"I don't know," he said.

"Well, as it turns out, it takes seven years for that to happen. It would be a lot shorter, except for your brain cells. They live the longest—about seven years. So every seven years, you suddenly have a completely different body, made up of completely different stuff. Nothing in your body today—not one thing—was there when you were born. Now if you are just your body, then you would feel like a completely different person today than you were then, wouldn't you?" I asked.

"Yes, but I don't."

"Do you think that you're the same person now that you were seven years ago?" I asked.

"Yes, I know I am," he said.

"I know I am, too," I said, "but my body has completely changed six times by now. So what do you think that means?"

"That I am something different than my body?" he offered. We were, I told myself, finally airborne; feet out of the water, arcing into the sky.

"Yes," I answered. "Christopher, your body is an important part of what you are, but it is not *all* that you are. If it were, then how could that woman you told me about see what her daughter was wearing back at her house, when she was lying in the hospital dead? There is a part of you that never changes and will always live, and it might go through twelve or fifteen different bodies while it is on this earth. It is your soul, and your soul is who you really are. You and I and everyone else are souls, souls on a long, long journey to learn how to love and to laugh and to grow together toward God. And even though the vehicle we use to get around in this world keeps changing, and even though we finally lay it aside because we don't need it anymore, that doesn't mean that *we* die. Do you see what I mean?"

With a stifled giggle and a bemused smile, he said, "Kind of reminds me of that time when we traded in the old car and got the new one."

"But that's exactly what it's like," I said. "That's such a good example, Christopher. You picked out the old car, remember?"

"Yes."

"What color did you pick? Do you remember that?" I asked.

"Heather Mist," he said.

"Heather Mist. You sure did like that car, didn't you?"

"Yeah—it was cool," he agreed.

"And when the lease was up, and we had to turn it in, you were kind of sad, weren't you?" I asked.

"Yes," he said, "I loved that car, and I was sure that I would really miss it, but I like the new one okay."

"Right," I said, "So do I. And we are both the same people we were, even though we aren't riding around in that Heather Mist Honda anymore, but a Huntsman Green one instead, right?"

"Oh, yeah," he said. A light was beginning to burn dimly in his head.

"And we are also the same people we were, even after we have switched into a whole new body every seven years," I said.

"But then we die," he added quickly.

"But then our *bodies* die, Christopher, and *we* keep on growing. God gives us whatever kind of

56

body we need for the next part of the journey, and we keep growing, and learning, and loving," I said.

"But we can't *see* that part of us. How do we know it's really there?" he asked.

"We can't see our soul, but we can feel it, and know that it's real; it's a lot like love that way," I said.

"How can I feel my soul?" Christopher asked.

"You have felt it a couple of times today already," I said.

"Oh," he said, "you mean riding in the boat?"

"And sky riding," I nodded. "Whenever you feel that happy and free, whenever you are filled with love, whenever you feel as though you are flying, or should be able to, that is your soul rejoicing to be alive, telling you what you're really made of. That is you, and you are never going to die. Not your soul. Not all that freedom and joy and love. Every once in a while, your soul sings out, and you feel it, and it reminds you of who you really are. Listen to it . . . feel it . . . pay attention to those moments. And remember them when they're gone, because they help you get to know yourself—who you really are down under that windblown bag of skin and bones."

"And my soul isn't going to die when my bag of bones does?" he asked with a giggle.

"No, Christopher," I reassured him, putting my arm around his precious bag of bones. "Your soul can never die, because it is made of the pure immortal energy of life, fashioned for you by God himself. We all get scared when we see somebody else's body die, because that is the only part of them we can see. And we're sad, because we know that we will never be able to see them in the same way that we have known them ever again. But that doesn't mean that they aren't still alive.

"Christopher, you are a child of God, made in God's own image, and that's a pretty amazing thing to be. Down underneath everything else you are, there is a soul that is made of pure energy and light. That is what you most truly *are*, and you will never die. God won't allow it. You will live on and on, here and there—wherever God wishes you to be—learning and growing in so many different ways and in so many different places. God loves you so much that you will never be alone for one single moment along the way; God's Spirit is within you, a part of you, to guide you and to remind you of who you really are, and to help you do remarkable things that you could never do on your own."

"Cool," said Christopher after a few seconds of reflection, and then: "Can we go get ice cream? I want a chocolate chip cookie dough cone with two scoops." Not exactly the kind of response I was expecting, but how boring life would be if everything happened just as we expected. Besides, I had the clear sense that our discussions were now airborne, and it felt right to celebrate.

So we finished walking the dog, and everyone piled into the car to go to the ice cream stand in the next town. Before we left the island road, the kids, sky riding up through the sunroof, started singing their favorite song of the summer for car rides, a Shari Lewis song called "The Song that Never Ends," modified to be "The Road that Never Ends":

This is the road that never ends,

It just goes on and on my friends;

Some people started drivin' it, not knowin' what it was,

And they'll just keep on drivin' it forever,

just because . . .

The entire thing is repeated, ad nauseum, until voices get tired or the road actually does stop. But on this trip, about four repetitions into the song, Christopher suddenly changed the words again; he led the whole carload of us in singing "The Life that Never Ends":

This is the life that never ends,
It just goes on and on my friends;
Some people started livin' it not knowin' what it was,
And they'll just keep on livin' it forever,
just because

This is the life that never ends,
It just goes on and on my friends;
Some people started livin' it not knowin' what it was,
And they'll just keep on livin' it forever,
just because . . .

He had all of us singing that new refrain loudly, over and over again, until we hit the ice cream stand. Christopher, I noticed with delight, had a big smile on his face, and it was obvious that he had more than mere chocolate chip cookie dough ice cream on his mind.

Death, be not proud,

though some have called thee

Mighty and dreadful, for thou art not so:

For those whom thou think'st thou dost

overthrow

Die not, poor Death, nor yet canst thou

kill me.

. . . One short sleep

past, we wake eternally,

And Death shall be no more:

Death, thou shalt die!

—John Donne[4]

FIVE

By the time the glorious, clear days of midsummer have graced our lakeside abode, the delicate blossoms of the lady's-slippers have long since dropped to the ground, and the bold hues of the iris have reached the end of their beauty's brief reign over the lakeshore. The wild blueberry bushes now take center stage along the waterfront, their shimmering dance in the afternoon breeze revealing the promise of a precious treasure yet to come: tiny immature berries of white and pink that will ripen with rain and the warmth of the sun to become the sweet blue fruit that will adorn muffins, pancakes, cereal, and shortcake in August.

On one such day we received word that my uncle had died, not an unexpected event after his long struggle with worsening emphysema and related problems. Hildreth Burton Woodward was his given name, explanation enough as to why everyone called him Woody. He was my mother's brother, as well as my godfather. His influence on me has been strong throughout my life, and my children knew and loved him, too. So when word came, and the funeral was scheduled in New Hampshire, we went without question to be there with his family. In the midst of getting ready to go, I didn't even think about how the prospect of attending a funeral might be affecting Chris. He was the one who let me know. After we got on the road, and while all the others in the car were engaged in a serious attempt to figure out the next correct Cat's Cradle move (their fingers hopelessly snagged in string), Christopher asked, "Do I have to go to this funeral, Dad, or can I stay outside?"

"We'll go to the funeral as a family, all of us," I said.

"But Dad, I've never been to a funeral, and because of the stuff I've been worrying about lately, I don't think it would be a very good thing for me to go," he said. "Don't you agree?"

How could I have missed this one? I asked myself. The poor guy was scared, which is something I should have anticipated before we headed out. He had never been to a funeral, and he was really worried about what the next couple of hours were going to bring.

"I'm sorry," I said. "Let's talk about the funeral. I think that you'll be very comfortable if you come to the service."

"Well, there's one thing I'm really worried about, Dad," he said.

"What's that?" I asked.

"When we go into the church, can we just sit right down?"

"We'll probably see other people that we know there and talk with them before the service begins, but then we'll go in and sit down, yes. What are you worried about?"

"I don't want to have to see his dead body."

"Nobody's going to see his body," I assured him. "Did you think that you would have to?"

"Yes. I mean, somebody told me once, I don't remember who it was, that at funerals everyone goes into the church, and they can't go and sit

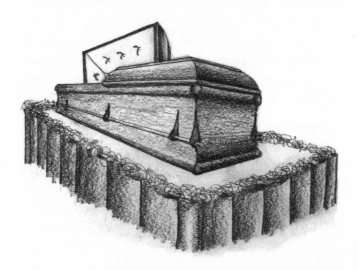

down until they go up to where the box is and look into it."

"The box? You mean the casket?"

"Yeah—the casket. I couldn't remember what they call that box they put you in."

"Some people are buried in caskets, and in some churches they let you go up and see the person's body if you want to," I told him. "But Uncle Woody was cremated, so there will probably be just a little urn with his ashes in it."

"Ashes? They made Uncle Woody into ashes? Is that what that word means?"

"Cremation?"

"Yes, cremation," he echoed.

"Cremation," I began, wondering how to explain this to a nine-year-old, "is when they take the person's body and burn it, so that there are just some ashes left, and then we bury the ashes in a cemetery just like a body, or sometimes people scatter the ashes over a place that the person really liked a lot."

"Do they ever burn people while they are still alive, by mistake?" Christopher asked.

"No; they make sure that the person is really dead first," I assured him, smiling.

"But what if they did? What if someone was so sick they thought he was dead, and they took him and started burning him up, and he woke up right then?"

"I don't think that could ever happen. They're pretty careful about that sort of thing."

"How do they do it? Do they put them in something like an oven?"

"It's sort of like an oven, but much bigger," I said, with growing concern about my ability to deal with the subject into which we were plunging. It wasn't enough for my son to be frightened of death in general; now he could add to that the specific fear of being burned up in a big oven after he died, or even before he died, straight out of the horrific fairy tale of Hansel and Gretel with the witch.

"Is there a window in it?" he asked.

"A window?" I said, confused.

"Yes; is there a window so that if the person wakes up when they turn on the oven, someone else will see them waving and turn the oven off and let them out?"

"Yes, Chris, I'm sure there is."

"Good," he said, with obvious relief. The presence of a window in the oven door seemed to take away all his anxiety about the prospect of being burned alive. Then, after a pause, "Can I see his ashes?"

"No," I said. "They are in some kind of an urn, a small container, so you can't see them."

"Oh, I see," he said, his face lighting up with fresh insight. "So the big difference is that if you are buried in your body in a box, everybody can come up to your box and see you if they want to. But if your body is burned up and just your ashes are up there, nobody can come up and see your ashes, even if they wanted to."

"Well, I guess that's one of the differences," I said with a chuckle.

"But that's not logical," Christopher responded matter-of-factly.

"Why not?"

"Because I would actually like to see Uncle Woody's ashes; they wouldn't frighten me at all," he continued, "but I would never want to see his dead body. It would be too scary for me. There are probably a lot of people out there just like me, and it isn't logical that they make us look at something so scary that we probably would have nightmares that night, but they won't let us see something that would be a lot more interesting, but not very scary."

As I tried to digest what he had just said, he continued, "Why would anyone want to have someone burn them up? Why would anyone want that to be done to them?"

"There are different reasons," I said. "Cemeteries are running out of room, and ashes take up just a little bit of space compared to a whole casket. Also, if you want your remains to be scattered in a special spot, or to be buried at sea, then your remains have to be ashes."

"I still wouldn't want them to do that to me," he said.

"Would they really be burning you?" I asked.

"Oh, yeah," he replied, remembering our previous discussion. "So Uncle Woody wasn't even there when they burned up his body, right?"

"Right."

"Do you think that he knew? Do you think that maybe he watched them burn his body?"

"Maybe," I said, imagining for a moment the relief and joy that my uncle must have felt to be liberated from that broken body that had become such a prison for him. "But I think he probably had more important things to be doing at the time."

We arrived at the church about a half-hour before the service was to begin, and we were directed to a side room in which family members were waiting. To get to the room, we first had to pass through the sanctuary. As we did so, Christopher focused on a small table at the front. On it was a walnut urn, with a folded

71

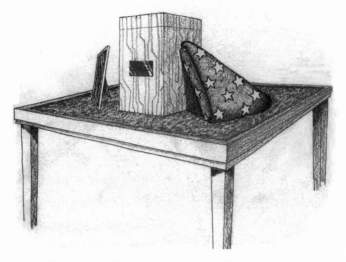

American flag leaning against it, and a photograph of Uncle Woody standing beside it.

"Are those his ashes?" he asked me in a whisper.

"Yes. They're in that wooden urn," I whispered back.

"Why is that flag there?"

"Because Uncle Woody was a veteran."

"What is a veteran?" he whispered. "Does that mean he was really old?"

"No," I said. "Uncle Woody was in the army in World War II. So the flag is there as a sign of the service he gave for his country."

I paused to reflect on that service; I had heard the story a number of times since childhood. Woody, a communications specialist, was in the front lines during the final invasion of Germany near the end of the war. His platoon came upon a German farmhouse that had come under a blistering German attack. A group of allied soldiers had defended their position from the basement of the house. In the firefight that followed, the farmhouse was reduced to rubble, and most of the soldiers in the basement were killed. Woody went into the basement alone to rescue one soldier still alive. Once inside, he encountered a toxic gas that rendered him unconscious. Both he and the soldier he went in to help had to be pulled out of the rubble, not regaining consciousness until about a half-hour later. He came home a hero, with a Purple Heart.

Once inside the family waiting room at the church, we all dispersed in various directions, each seeking out a particular cousin, uncle, or aunt. Christopher was silent, and when I sat down on a couch on one side of the room, he sat right next to me, looking apprehensive. The room was full of Woody's four children and his grandchildren, everybody talking, and many people laughing.

"Dad?" Christopher said, pulling on my sleeve.

"What?"

"Most of these people are smiling and having a good time. Are they *happy* that Uncle Woody is dead?"

73

"No, of course not," I said. "Everybody here loved Uncle Woody very much."

"Then why are they laughing and smiling and telling jokes at his funeral?" he asked.

"Well, we're not at the funeral yet. We're just in here while we wait. And it's been so long since we have seen all of these cousins, that everyone is excited to see each other, and they're having a good time. There's nothing wrong with that. The other reason that it's okay is that we all know that Uncle Woody is just fine. He had been so sick for such a long time, and it's a big relief that he's not stuck in that sick old body anymore. We're sure going to miss him, but it helps to know that God is taking care of him now, and that he's not going to be sick anymore."

"Are they going to act that way in the church?" he asked, obviously trying to gauge just how far this merrymaking was going to go.

"No, I'm sure they're not," I assured him.

And they didn't act that way during the service, of course. Lined up and led into the church, we walked up the center aisle toward the reserved pews in the front, with Christopher gripping my hand more tightly with each step. There was a nice opening hymn, some prayers, and readings from Scripture. Then the minister began his homily from the pulpit:

74

"Death is not something we like to talk about much in our society. In fact, just thinking about the prospect that you and I and everyone else in this world are going to die one day terrifies us. We want so desperately to understand this thing called death . . ."

I looked over at Christopher and saw that he was sitting up straight, his eyes and ears riveted to the man in the pulpit. "Sounds like he's talking to you," I whispered into Christopher's ear. He nodded, still listening intently, while the preacher went on to speak about people's love for Woody and quoted several Bible passages in which we are promised that eternal life is waiting for us after death. After the sermon I led some prayers, and Christopher's younger cousin Kimberly stood in front of the congregation and sang a song about the triumph of life over death, her beautiful, strong voice carrying throughout the church. Woody's eldest son, Kurt, rose to speak of his dad in eloquent words that acknowledged both the glory and the pain of his father's life. More prayers, another hymn, and the service was over.

On the way to the reception after the service, I asked Christopher if he had been comfortable with the funeral service. He said that he had actually enjoyed it; the music, the preaching, and his seeing his cousins read lessons and sing songs all had made the experience much more uplifting than he had anticipated. The service had been a celebration of life. I was pleased for Christopher's sake that it had been so, considering some of the alternatives that I had encountered over the years.

"And best of all," Chris added, "was that I didn't even have to look at his dead body." With that criterion satisfied, my nine-year-old judged the day a success.

All goes onward and outward,
nothing collapses,
And to die is different from what
anyone supposed,
and luckier . . .

They are alive and well
somewhere,
The smallest sprout shows there is
really no death,
And if there ever was, it led forward
life,
and does not wait at the end to
arrest it,
And ceas'd the moment life appeared.

—Walt Whitman[5]

SIX

Later the same evening, funeral and reception behind him, Christopher approached me while we were all getting ready for bed. "You know, Mom's grandfather died just a few days before I was born," he said.

"Yes," I answered. "He was very sick, but he was so excited that your mother was about to give birth to his first great-grandchild. The doctor said that he thought he was just trying to stay alive in order to hear the news that you were finally here."

"But he didn't, did he?" Christopher said.

"No. He gave it his best shot, but he finally had to leave just before you arrived."

"Mom said that she couldn't go to his funeral. She would have, but I was supposed to be born right when the funeral happened. Did you know him?"

"Oh yes," I said, "I got to see him several times; he was a wonderful man, and he would have been very proud of you. You know, on the Sunday after you were born, I preached a sermon about Granddaddy dying and you being born. It was a sermon about you and him, and it was also about life and death."

"It was?" said Christopher. "Could I read it sometime?"

"Sure you can. I wrote it for you; I guess it's about time you saw it."

As I went to get my laptop computer, my mind recalled the circumstances under which that sermon had been written. Sharra, Christopher's mother, had been experiencing intermittent contractions throughout the night, but they were not regular. We lay in bed recording the exact time of each contraction, unable to sleep with the excitement of what was undoubtedly soon to come. Finally, at about one o'clock on the morning of Friday, February 3, 1989, a set of contractions that seemed serious settled in, and they repeated, like clockwork, at first five-, and then four-, and then three-minute intervals. We called the doctor, who just happened to be on the maternity ward at the hospital delivering babies, and he asked us to come on over. We arrived at around three, and Christopher was born at about five. Then the party started, or at least as much of a party as two exhausted new parents could manage. We took turns holding the baby, oohing and aahing and crying and laughing all at the same time. Next came the ritual of telephone calls, following a rigid protocol that we had previously agreed on, a list that dictated which relatives would receive the first calls. All of that took another couple of hours, after which we oohed and aahed and cried and laughed again, until suddenly my entire body turned to lead, and I became aware that it was taking an enormous amount of effort just to keep my eyes open, and even more to stand up. I was exhausted, and therefore I could only guess at Sharra's level of fatigue. So the nurses took Christopher to the nursery, Sharra settled down for a nap, and I went home to get some sleep as well.

I arrived home at about eleven o'clock in the morning. Walking into the house, I took off my coat, and then, without thinking, sat down at my computer and began to write. I sat at that desk and wrote continuously for well over an hour, after which I went upstairs, collapsed in bed, and did not rise again until later that evening. When I awoke, I lay in bed reliving the past twenty-four hours in my mind with deep joy. I recalled that I had written something when I arrived home, but despite my best effort, I could not remember what it was or why I had written it. Not one little bit. Wondering, then, whether my memory of sitting at the computer might have been merely a dream, I rushed downstairs to my desk, turned on the computer, and found a new document in my "sermons" file; it was a sermon written for the following Sunday, just two days away. I had been agonizing over what to preach that week; the Gospel lesson was the story of the Transfiguration of Jesus on the mountaintop, and I had preached on that subject so many times that I just couldn't think of something new to say about it. I opened the new document in my computer and began to read in total wonderment; even as I read the sermon, I still could not remember having written any part of it just a few hours earlier:

> One of the things that sets us apart from the rest of the animal kingdom is our innate need to make sense out of the life in which we find ourselves. We have the unique and yet frustrating ability to transcend ourselves—step outside of ourselves—and analyze the context of our lives; frustrating, because more often than not, we do not possess the breadth of vision necessary to see "the whole picture."And that can leave us confused and embittered about just what the rules are to this whole game of life. So often, what we see happening to us and around us doesn't seem fair. And yet in those same times,

what we see is but a fraction of the evidence we would need to make a valid judgment of fairness or unfairness. Nowhere does the frustration become greater than in the paradox of life and death. Two realities over which we have no control, under which we all become subservient; life and death both have dominion over us, and we have little if any understanding of either of them. To the gift of life we call ourselves heirs; to the inevitable grip of death we call ourselves victims. When we try to look at those two realities together—as a package deal—we see ourselves at best as pawns; brought into this world from who knows where, by unknown forces, and then, when we can least predict it, forced to exit this arena of earthly life to a destination of which we have hardly a glimpse, and certainly no comprehension.

Life and death; death and life. These two mysteries have thrust themselves upon my family with full impact recently.

Just a couple of weeks ago, Sharra's grandfather died. His name was James Kelly, and he was eighty-nine years old. After his death, many referred to him as "the last of the Virginia Gentlemen," and that appraisal may in fact be true. I had the distinct privilege of meeting this man a number of times over the past few years, and I found him to be a rare combination of quiet wisdom, rock-solid steadiness of character, impeccable manners, and abundant compassion and love. Though eighty-nine, his departure from this dimension of life was a sudden blow; ongoing trouble with his blood for a couple of years had turned into a form of leukemia that over-powered him within a matter of days. The sadness and grief of losing one who has been such a touchstone for so many for so long simply cannot be described. With that passing, a void is left in people's lives that can never really be filled again. And that void seems to just fill up with questions, all the usual questions: Why . . . ? What if . . . ? Where . . . ?

Then, just two days ago, at 5:00 A.M., there pops into our lives and into our world a little boy by the name of Christopher Sands Dugan. He had been long awaited by a number of people. Indeed, James Kelly, his great-grandfather, had mentioned on a daily basis near the end that he just wanted to live to see his great-grandchild.

That joyful meeting was not to be, not in this plane of existence anyway. But, just as I had met his great-grandfather before him, I have also had the privilege of meeting Christopher a few times by now, and I find him to be the very embodiment of gentle innocence and love placed into our care by a God who knew how desperately his new parents yearned to have a child to nurture and to love. That such a perfect creation could have only come from God seems obvious to me, though I do not understand it. It remains truly a holy mystery before which I bow in grateful humility. And after just two days with him, Sharra and I cannot imagine our lives without him.

Having been caught up in these recent events, it should come as no surprise to anyone that the mystery of life and death has been something which has weighed heavily on my mind of late. I cannot tell you this morning that I have any new answers to the mystery, but I do want to share a different perspective.

Imagine for a moment that you and I lived in a womb—a woman's womb. It is a small place, but it is the full range of our perception. We have heard that there is a much larger, brighter, better world that lies very close at hand, but we cannot see this other world, nor do we have access to it. Now think what it would be like to watch another presence take shape in our world. A beautiful, perfect little life grows in purest contentment over the space of nine months. We can lay no claim to this new life; it is not ours, though it definitely has become part of our world over that time. You could say that after some time we have come to take its presence for granted. Now, imagine just a little further: A moment comes when our world becomes seemingly hostile. The warm water in which this baby has been gently floating all of its life is suddenly poured out. The walls beyond the water come to life, and press in on every side, pushing the child down so that its squeezed head disappears from view. And we cry out in our powerlessness and frustration, "What is happening? What kind of God could create something so perfect only to do this to it? Is our God a God who gets some kind of sadistic pleasure out of the obvious suffering of such an innocent child?" In a final moment of intensely convulsive horror, the child is gone, and all that remains is darkness, and memories of one we came to love, and, worst of all, stunned confusion. For all we have seen is an ending, and a violent one at that.

We cannot see the tears of joy just outside, nor the loving arms that are holding and caressing the child as it begins a newer, greater form of existence. Our ears cannot hear the words of love that are gently bestowed, nor the expressions of awe and wonder at where such a perfect, beautiful creation could possibly have come from. Our vision cannot reach even the short distance necessary to see the one we loved drawing new warmth and sustenance from its mother's breast in purest contentment and quiet joy.

Imagining such a thing, I think perhaps that is the vantage point we find ourselves taking when we watch someone slip away from this earthly life through death. In a few moments we will profess our faith in the reality of things "seen and unseen" in the Nicene Creed. We can easily believe in the things that we see. Science is telling us more every day about how many things there are that we cannot see. The things unseen are held in belief by faith, intuition, and common sense. To believe in things unseen is not a psychological crutch, nor is it a rationalization of a meaningless existence. It is rather an acknowledgment that the universe in which we exist is a far greater expanse of reality than we will ever have access to in this lifetime. It is an acknowledgment that God is good, and wise, and loving, and far more capable and powerful than all of us put together.

There is an anonymous piece of writing called "The Horizon." It reads as follows:

You are standing upon the seashore. A ship at your side spreads her white sails in the morning breeze and starts for the blue ocean.

She is an object of beauty and strength, and you stand and watch her until at length she hangs like a speck of white cloud just where the sea and sky come down to mingle with each other.

Then someone at your side says, "There, she's gone!" Gone where?

Gone from your sight—that is all.

She is just as large in mast and hull and spar as she was when she left your side. Just as able

90

to bear her load of living freight to the place of destination.

Her diminished size is in you, not in her. And just at the moment when someone at your side says, "There, she's gone," there are other eyes watching her coming, and other voices ready to take up the glad shout, "Here she comes!"

That is what we mean when we say that death is only a horizon.

James Kelly, I believe in the Communion of Saints; I believe that you and the rest of that "great cloud of witnesses" can see and hear me even now. Your passing from us is greatly mourned, for there are so many who love you. But your laboring out of this world meant for you a new birth into the next, which by God's infinite grace you are growing into more fully and completely each day. Your life in this earthly dimension was lived out with integrity, compassion, patience, and love. You can be proud of that, for to those whose lives touched yours most closely, you passed on a legacy of honor and truth which will be perpetuated for a long time to come. The world is in dire need of the gentle, quiet wisdom that you personified. The little child for whom you waited with all your remaining strength: It is a boy, named Christopher. And he will most assuredly reap the benefits of your legacy, for you taught and nurtured your son, and he has now become a grandfather, just as you were one. He will love this precious new child with his whole being, and he will teach by his strong, quiet, and loving example, just as you once did. And because of that, a part of you will always be within your great-grandson.

And to Christopher, as he begins his earthly journey, I would say this: You have just labored your way into a new life. Your mother and I were there to welcome you, and we will love you and nurture you as long as we are able. But someday the time will probably come when you will have to see us leave, just as we saw you arrive. Remember then that the only absolute in entering this paradoxical life is that one day you must leave it behind; along with the gift of life goes the certainty of having to give it back again and journeying on anew. So when we have left, please take whatever we gave you that was good and right and true and pass it on—it's probably from one of your grandparents or great-grand-parents. At that same time, please also forgive us for whatever we gave you that was hurtful, for we will most certainly never do that intentionally. But be aware of what it was, so that you do not pass it on. And know in your heart as you miss us that you have seen us labor our way into a newer, brighter existence and that there are many divinely radiant souls on the other side to welcome us, souls who have passed on before us, one of them undoubtedly named James Kelly.

I want my son to know from the outset that, whatever we think of it, whatever it seems, this is a place that we pass through. We are borne into it by the wind of God's own Spirit. And sooner or later all of us set our sails once again and are carried by that same loving breeze on to our next destination. The journey is an eternal one. None of us is victim. Each of us is heir, heir to the richness and fullness of the whole created order, even the parts we cannot yet see.

And whatever our questions or confusion as we journey through, we need look only one place to quiet our racing hearts, to calm our anxiety. We need to look at the figure in our Gospel reading today, a lone man standing at the top of a mountain. He stands there looking over the landscape of time, his eyes full of God's own wisdom, his raiment dazzling, shining brighter than the sun. His vision stretches far beyond our own, and he alone directs the winds that fill our sails and carry us on. . . .

As Christopher slowly scrolled through "his" sermon on my computer, pausing to clarify the meaning of a word with me now and then, I sat quietly beside him, watching. In my mind an image kept reasserting itself: This sermon was like a message in a bottle, floating over the ocean of time until this moment. *How amazing*, I thought, *that the very subject about which I wrote at his birth should have resurfaced as his principle anxiety nine years later. Or was it because he was born into that very tension that it resurfaced now?* It didn't really matter; Chris finished reading, turned to me, and said, "That's really awesome, Dad, that you wrote that for me, when you didn't even know that I'd be wondering about this same thing nine years later. You know what I mean?"

You shall ask
What good are dead leaves
And I will tell you
They nourish the sore earth.
You shall ask
What reason is there for winter
And I will tell you
To bring about new leaves.
You shall ask
Why are the leaves so green
And I will tell you
Because they are rich with life.
You shall ask
Why must summer end
And I will tell you
So that the leaves can die.

—Nancy Wood[6]

SEVEN

One of the prices that we pay for the isolation and natural beauty of our lake is a forty-minute drive to the nearest grocery store. We stock up as much as we can when we're there, but about once a week it becomes necessary to make the drive, either to get more groceries, take a pile of laundry to the laundromat, or both. One such moment of necessity came just as my sister and her husband had arrived for a few days with their toddler, Emma. Normally, all four children make a beeline to the car when they hear that such an expedition is being mounted, but on this particular day their cousin Emma stole their hearts; they wanted to stay and play with her. I walked to the car with some anticipation, relishing the prospect of three or more hours by myself. I could listen to the classical radio station turned up loud without complaints from the back seat. Or I could turn off the radio if I wanted and just drive in blissful silence. There would be no fights erupting in the back seat about who was taking up the most room. I could stroll through the grocery store without my small committee of shopping consultants making it their objective to get me to buy at least twice what was on my list. I got into the car, closed the door, turned on the ignition, turned on the radio, and smiled as I took in a deep breath of fresh Maine air and put the car in reverse. Then, turning my head around to back out of the driveway, I noticed the passenger in the back seat.

"Dad, is it okay if I go with you? I wanted to stay and play with Emma, too, but when I realized that you were going alone, I thought it might be a good time for another lesson," Christopher said. I turned off the radio.

"Another lesson?" I asked. "Right now?" All of my fantasies regarding the next three hours were colliding head-on with this unexpected passenger.

"It might be our only chance to talk in the next few days, Dad, and I have some more questions I really want to ask you," he said. He was right, of course; with company, things would be busier than usual in the coming days.

"Okay, my friend. Welcome aboard," I said, and we were off.

After spending a few minutes comparing our impressions of how much Emma had grown since we had last seen her, I asked Christopher what he wanted to discuss. He paused for a few moments to collect his thoughts, and then he stated matter-of-factly, "First, I have to ask you a few things about the Bible."

"Okay," I said. "Shoot."

"First of all," Christopher began, "it's the Bible that tells us that there is a God and that He promises us there is a place called heaven that we go to when we die, but how do we know that's all true? I mean, it's just a book, right, and anybody can write a book."

"Well, it's not really just another book, Christopher," I said. "And it's not really a book, either."

"It's not?"

"No, the Bible is a collection of more than sixty different books, all coming from different times and different places, and written by different people. The Bible is actually more like a library. And it is a library that has been carefully preserved and translated into different languages for hundreds and even thousands of years now. So it's not like some other book that someone may have just written a couple of years ago. Do you see what I mean?"

"Yes, but whenever each of the books was written, it was a person who wrote it, right?" he asked.

"Of course," I said. "Why?"

"Because I have friends at school who say that God wrote the Bible, and that I have to do everything it says or I won't go to heaven when I die. But I don't see how God could have sat down and written anything. I think that different people wrote it, and I don't see how I can trust what they say; they might just be making it all up."

"You're right. They could be making it all up," I said. "Nowhere in the Bible does it say that God wrote it. In fact, almost every book of the Bible tells you the name of the person who wrote that book. But everywhere in the Bible it says very clearly that the people who wrote those books felt that they were *inspired* by God."

"Inspired? You mean when they thought about God it made them feel really good?" he asked.

"Yes, but much, much more than that," I answered quickly. "When we say that they were inspired by God, we mean that they were people who for very different reasons had all come very close to God, so close that they could almost see and feel and smell and taste God; that's how close they had come. And it wasn't that they were all looking for God. In fact, most of them, from Moses at the beginning to Saint John at the end, were just ordinary people, not looking for anything like what actually happened to them. And some of them, like Jonah with the whale, were scared of God, and tried to run away, because they saw how amazingly huge and powerful God was. But all of them came so close that they learned something about God, something so important that they felt that they just *had* to sit and write it down, so that other people could know about the part of God that they had experienced. And now, after thousands of years of certain people doing that, we have a collection of their different experiences of God, each experience giving another little or big detail of who this God is that people sense is there but want to know more about. And we have put this collection into one book, so that by putting all these different accounts together, a much larger picture of who God really is could be seen, like putting together different pieces of a jigsaw puzzle, you know? The frustrating thing for you and me is that the Bible is like a jigsaw puzzle of a lighthouse that has a lot of pieces missing. When we put the available pieces together, we can see an overall picture and know some of the general information about it, like that it is a picture of a lighthouse. But we can't see a lot of the little details that we would really like to know about it yet, such as what kind of land it is built on because those pieces aren't yet in place. Does that make any sense to you?"

"Oh yeah," he said, having recently proven himself one of the fastest jigsaw puzzle assemblers in the family. "Like when I was looking for the tree trunk piece." In the last puzzle, an outdoor scene, Christopher was trying to find all the pieces that comprised a tree trunk. One piece about halfway up the tree was missing. He was increasingly frustrated, because there were no more pieces left that had any of that tree trunk on them. He didn't look at any of the other remaining pieces, because he knew it wouldn't have been "logical" to put any other kind of piece in there. The tree trunk was straight and thick and brown at the bottom, and the same way up at the top. So the middle of the trunk must be just the same, he reasoned. As it turned out, the missing piece just happened to contain all of the green foliage on a branch from another tree *crossing in front of* the tree trunk he was trying to complete. While he had been looking for a brown piece, the actual piece that fit was almost totally green.

"Exactly," I said to him. "The Bible is like that puzzle; there are enough pieces to give us a pretty good idea of how huge and powerful and wonderful God can be, but we are missing just a few of the pieces that would give us some of those details that we want. So we decide what we *think* those missing pieces would show about God if they were in place. Different people have different opinions about it, and they even end up fighting sometimes, fighting over something about which no one really has a clear answer."

"Like reincarnation?" Christopher offered.

"Yes," I said. "Reincarnation is one of those. That's actually a good example, because the leaders of the church argued about it hundreds of years ago, and people still don't agree about it today. It's one of those missing pieces in the Bible. Over the centuries, some people have said that Jesus taught that reincarnation was true, and some have said that he didn't. It's very difficult to say who is right, because the New Testament really doesn't mention it one way or the other."

The subject had arisen earlier in the day, down on the dock, as we all lay in the sun trying to warm our shivering bodies after a swim. Lying flat on his stomach to avoid the cool breeze, Christopher had called across to me, "What *are* these things?"

"What things?"

"These *dead* things—I see them everywhere."

Crawling over to his side of the dock, I followed his gaze and pointing finger to the side of the dock, where a couple of gray, empty husks with the appearance of spiders still clung to the wood. Gaping holes blew outward from the center of their backs.

"They look like little tiny *Alien* monsters," Chris said. "You know, in the movie, when the baby alien comes out of that guy's chest? Except here it has come out of the back of these things."

"Those are dragonfly nymphs," I said. "They crawl around like big spiders until the day comes

106

when a hole splits open in their back, and out comes a big, beautiful dragonfly, with two big sets of wings."

"That's where dragonflies come from?" he said with amazement. "That's so awesome; they get to be two completely different things! First they're like a spider, and then they can fly around with four huge wings. It's just like butter-flies; they start out as a caterpillar, and then they turn into butterflies. That's what some people say *we* do; what's that word, when we come back as somebody different?"

"*Reincarnation?*" I asked.

107

"Yeah . . . reincarnation," he had repeated in a distant voice, springing to his feet in the next instant to try to net a turtle that was swimming too close to the dock.

The subject had obviously been gestating in his mind ever since.

"There is a guy at school I was talking to who says that when we die, we go to heaven, and then come right back to earth; and then we die again and go to heaven, and then come right back to earth. Heaven, earth, heaven, earth, heaven, earth; I think that I would just get tired of the whole thing if that's all I was doing, don't you?" he asked.

"If I remembered it all," I said. "But what if each time you came to earth you came without a very clear memory of where you had been and what you had done before? What if it was so important to keep all of your attention on the job of learning and growing here and now that you came without much memory of what you had done in the past?"

"So you would do a better job?" he asked.

"Uh-huh," I answered. "When you are in school listening to the teacher or reading something, how much time do you spend thinking about being up here at the lake in the summer?"

"Well, I try not to," he said, a grin forming on his face, "because when I do that, I can't keep my mind on what I'm supposed to be doing, and I just think about fishing and swimming and all that stuff instead."

"Right," I said. "So can you imagine what it would be like to try to study your multiplication tables or keep your attention on anything else that you have to do if you remembered already having been here a bunch of times?"

Chris pondered that one for a while, and then asked, "What do you think about it, Dad?"

"About reincarnation?"

"Yes," he said, "Do you think we keep coming back here?"

With the directness of his question he had cornered me with a dilemma that afforded me only two possible responses. The first, of course, would be an answer that represented the Church's standard doctrinal response: "No, Christopher, as Christians we don't believe in reincarnation." That stock answer is based on the rulings of two Church Councils: the first at Lyons in 1274, and the second in Florence in 1439. In both instances, the issue of reincarnation, or *metempsychosis* as the Church has always referred to it, was of secondary or even tertiary importance on the agenda. Moreover, these rulings

109

were made in the midst of what was arguably the most embarrassing and shameful period in the history of Christianity. Following close on the heels of the Crusades, this was the time period of the Inquisition, during which thousands were barbarically tortured and killed in the name of Jesus Christ. It was the time of the Church's insistence, in the face of clear evidence to the contrary, that the earth, not the sun, was at the center of the solar system; Copernicus was censured and Galileo was dragged before the Inquisition. It was a time in which it was illegal to translate Scripture into any language other than Latin, lest the Church lose its power over people's minds. Shortly after these rulings, William Tyndale was strangled and burned at the stake simply because he had translated the Bible into English so that people could read it themselves. In light of the ignorance and barbarity running rampant within the Church during that period, I'm afraid that I have never been able to place much credibility in *anything* the Church said then, including two relatively minor statements on reincarnation.

So I opted to walk the second avenue with my son, that of personal honesty.

"I think that there is a chance that we do come back again," I said. "But none of us will know for sure until we leave this earth and find out. The one thing that I do know for sure is that God has designed a wonderful, mysterious way for us to live and learn and grow. When we are finished with this particular lifetime on earth, God will have things ready for us so that we can continue to grow and learn in just the way that is right for us. If that means coming back here again, fine. If it means staying in heaven forever, that's fine with me, too, because I know that wherever God puts me next is going to be the very best place for me to continue growing, so I don't need to spend my time worrying about it."

We were pulling into the grocery store parking lot at that moment, and I said, "Right now, the best chance we have to continue growing in *this* lifetime is to go in here and get some groceries." So in we went, scouring the store for everything on our list and some other things that we thought we might need in the course of the following week. The weather was supposed to be sunny and warm throughout the next several days, so I didn't want to have to make the long trip to the store again too soon. About an hour later, grocery bags filling the back of the car, we started home, and Christopher jumped right back into the discussion, wanting to use every moment available to him.

"Dad, what about heaven?" he asked. "The Bible says a lot about heaven, doesn't it?"

"Different books in the Bible do speak of heaven, a very different and wonderful kind of life that God has prepared for us, a kind of life that will never end, and is so different from the lives we have here on earth that there are not even words that can describe it," I said.

"Where is heaven?" Christopher asked.

"Nowhere, and everywhere," I said with a little smile, wondering how he would handle this one.

"Dad," he admonished me, "no place can be nowhere and everywhere at the same time."

"But heaven isn't a place," I said, only confusing him further.

"How can we go to heaven when we die if it's not even a real place?" he asked, his voice getting louder with frustration.

"It's not a place in the same way that we think of places," I tried to explain. "We're told that God lives outside of both space and time, and at the same time fills all of space and all of time. Even Jesus says that "the kingdom of heaven is in the midst of you." Heaven is all around us, everywhere, all the time, but it is not a place, not in the same way that our lake is a place that we can show somebody on a map and give them directions on how to get there. That's confusing, isn't it?"

"Yes," he said, "it's very confusing."

"Sorry," I said. "Heaven is one of those parts of the big picture puzzle where there are some pieces missing. But the important thing for us, I think, is to be able to know that God has it all under control; even if we don't understand it completely, God does, and part of our faith in God is the trust that, when the time comes, heaven will be there for us, and it will be more wonderful than anything we have ever known."

"Then what about hell?" came the inevitable question. "I have a friend at school who says that I'm going to go to hell because I don't go to the same church that he goes to. Is that true?"

"No, Christopher, that is not true," I said emphatically. "One really sad thing about Christianity is that it has used far too much fear over the years to get people to believe and attend church. However boring church might be, if you think that you are going to go to hell if you don't go to church, then going to church is probably what you will do. And sometimes people who go to one kind of church, but want everyone else to believe the same things that they do, will say that their church is the only church that God likes, and so if you don't go to that particular kind of church, then God will be angry at you and throw you into hell when you die."

113

"That's what my friend said to me," Chris said.

"Do you think that somebody who was a real friend of yours would tell you that you're going to end up in hell forever because you don't go to the same church as he does?" I asked.

"No," he said quietly.

"Do you think that God wants you to go to church and worship him just because you are afraid that he's going to punish you if you don't?"

"No," he said again.

"Don't you think that a God who loves you more than you can ever imagine, a God who made you in his own image and wants only the best for you, a God who understands that you are not perfect and that you're going to make mistakes once in a while, don't you think that a God like that would rather have you go to church because you *want* to? Wouldn't that mean more to God?"

"I guess so," he said.

"Would you like to have friends who were only nice to you because they were afraid that you would punish them forever if they didn't come to your house and visit you every week?" I asked.

"No," he said with a chuckle, "That would be stupid."

"Well," I said, "God thinks that's stupid, too. God is always going to love you, no matter what you think or do, just the way your mom and I love you. And God wants you to love him because you are so grateful for everything he has given you, not fear him because you think he's going to throw you into hell."

"But is there a hell?"

"Yes. But just like heaven, it's not a place, and it's not something which people live only after they die. Heaven and hell are two completely different ways of living life, and as we go through life, all of us make choices about which one we want to live, heaven or hell. But we start living them now; we can live in heaven or in hell while we are still walking this earth, and those decisions we have made go with us when we leave."

"What is hell?" he asked me.

"The Greek word the New Testament uses for hell is *gehenna*, and *gehenna* is a word that simply means 'chaos.' God gave us all freedom of choice to live the way we want to. That means we can choose to live closely with God, who, ever since the beginning of creation, has brought order to the universe. Inviting God to be a part of your life, something God wants more than anything, brings order and harmony and

115

real joy to life; you can start living a little bit of heaven right now. On the other hand, if you want to try to live your life on your own, without God's help, then God will stay out of your life, even though he still loves you very much. It's just that your life without God will tend to be pretty bumpy and disordered, and none of it will seem to make much sense. That's the beginning of life in hell: chaos. But whether our lives on earth are lived in heavenly ways or hellish ways is our decision to make."

"You mean *we* decide whether we're going to live in heaven or not?" Christopher asked. "I thought only *God* decided that."

"God loves us always, no matter what we do," I said. "And he wants every single one of us to live in heaven. But God has given us the freedom to make our own decisions about what kind of life we're going to live. There's a story about heaven and hell that I really like; it sort of explains what I'm trying to say.

"Once there was a man who died and appeared before the gates of heaven. His guardian angel welcomed the radiant soul of this man and opened the door to lead him in. The man interrupted him and said, 'Excuse me, but before we go in, could I please see hell? Heaven will mean so much more to me, I think, if I see what the alternative is.' The angel smiled, and led the man on a short walk to another door. Entering the door, the man gasped in surprise. Before him, and stretching out as far as his eyes could see, was a banquet table, loaded with every conceivable kind of food. But seated at the table were emaciated, starving people whose only implements for eating were four-foot-long chopsticks. Everyone was desperately grasping at the abundant food with their chopsticks, but they simply could not get the food into their mouths, and so they sat in this sad state of star-vation for all eternity, bickering and arguing with each other constantly. The man shuddered at the sight, and said to his guardian angel, 'I've seen enough. Now take me into heaven.'

"A short walk later, the angel pulled open the gate to heaven. In astonishment, the man noticed that the scene was virtually the same: A long banquet table stretched as far as the eye could see. The table was loaded with delicious food, and countless thousands of people were seated on either side of the table. Here, too, the only implements for eating were four-foot-long chopsticks. But here, in heaven, all the people were healthy and happy; they were singing and talking and laughing, and looked as though they were getting plenty of nourishment. The new arrival looked at his guide and said, 'I don't understand; how can this be? It looks like the very same place.' The angel said, 'It is the same place; all of God's children are welcomed into His heavenly banquet. The only difference is that here in heaven, we feed each other.'

"That's what heaven is really all about, Christopher—thinking of others more than yourself. Jesus said that we should love God and love our neighbor; if you do those two things, you can begin to live in heaven right now."

Just then the traffic in front of us stopped. As we inched ahead slowly, I soon could make out the figure of a police officer redirecting traffic. Cars were pulling off on the shoulder, and heading into an automobile dealership parking lot, where most of them were turning around and coming out, heading back in the opposite direction. Once we reached the police officer, the cause of the delay became apparent; down the other side of the hill we had been ascending was an accident involving two cars and a truck. Ambulances, fire trucks, and police cars crowded the road, making it impassable. The state trooper told me the road would be closed for at least another hour while they helped the injured and cleared the wreckage. We pulled into the car dealership and parked next to a minivan whose passengers were all standing outside. A distraught mother was trying to settle her four elementary-age children, each of whom seemed to be whining and pulling on some part of her clothing and asking her when they were going to get on the road again. As I got out of the car, she told me that she was here from Connecticut on vacation and had no idea where any of the roads went. Was there another road that could get her to the same destination? I said no, realizing for the first time that Chris and I were actually stuck here until they cleared the accident off the road. My very next thought was of all our family and the special dinner that was waiting for us back at the lake, a dinner timed to be ready at just about the time we should be returning. The next thought that entered my mind was the one that bothered me the most: I had ice cream in those plastic bags that were piled in the back of my warm car sitting in the late afternoon sun.

First things first: I called back to the lake on my cell phone and told them not to wait for us for dinner. My next concern was where Chris and I were going to get some supper ourselves. We sat in the car and discussed the fast-food outlets we had passed since leaving the grocery store; we didn't have much enthusiasm for any of

119

them. So we sat, watching how everyone else was coping with this little unexpected intermission in their lives. Some were not coping well. Christopher was particularly fascinated with a really "bad" character in a big souped-up sixties' Plymouth convertible. The young man would alternately rev his large, hardly muffled engine, and then walk up to the state trooper in the road and pressure him to let him drive past the wreckage. This routine repeated itself several times, until the officer finally told the guy to get out of the road and leave him alone. The frustrated man walked back to his machine and tore out of the parking lot and back down the road in the direction from which we had all come, making as much noise with his car as possible to register his displeasure. It was as we were laughing and noting how relatively quiet it had suddenly become that I happened to look in my rear-view mirror.

"Sometimes," I said to Christopher, "a piece of the puzzle can be sitting right in front of your nose and you don't see it, because you aren't expecting to see it there."

"What do you mean?" he asked.

"Well," I said, "you and I have been sitting here for several minutes trying to decide where we should get some supper. Look right behind us."

Christopher turned his head around and we both started to laugh, for there, right behind us, in the same parking lot, was a Chinese restaurant. Chinese food is one of Christopher's favorite things. Laughing at our oversight, we went into the restaurant. I was still worrying about our ice cream, so I asked the hostess if they had a freezer. The sweet, hospitable woman did not speak English very well, and she responded to me that the air conditioning was on, and if I was too warm she could turn the temperature down a little. No, I said, the temperature was fine. I told her that I had ice cream that was melting in my car. Yes, she said, they had ice cream on the menu. Yes, I said, but I wanted to put my ice cream in her freezer so that it wouldn't melt. Yes, she assured me, they kept their ice cream in a freezer, so it was fresh and delicious and frozen when served. I gave up. I asked her to take Christopher to our table, and said that I would be right back.

Running out to the car, I rummaged through the pile of plastic bags until I found all the ice cream. The stranded mother and her four young children were still standing next to our car, and by the sounds of the whining, I guessed that things were not getting better. "Have they had supper?" I asked her. "Yes," she said. I opened a box of ice cream sandwiches and asked if anyone wanted one. Instantly, eight hands stopped pawing their mother and four whines turned to one, loud, synchronous "Yes" as they ran over to me and took the ice cream sandwiches out of the box, giving back a quick "Thank you" for each one. A smile blossomed on their mother's face as she leaned back against her car and offered a very sincere "Thank you."

Back in the restaurant, I approached the hostess once again, this time with my soft ice cream in hand. "This is my ice cream," I said. "Do you have room for it in your freezer, so it won't melt?" I asked her. She let out a scream of delight and laughed as I asked her, now recognizing what I had been trying to tell her earlier. "Yes, I take," she said, and carried our ice cream off to the kitchen. From that point on, every time she came to our table she would laugh and say, "You ask about *your* ice cream. I think you ask about *our* ice cream!" and we would all laugh together one more time.

Chris ordered egg drop soup, and we decided that we would share some shrimp fried rice and sweet and sour chicken. Chris lost no time in starting right in on the pot of hot Chinese green tea, one of his favorite drinks, that been brought to the table. As he tried to cool both his tea and his soup, blowing on both of them, he said to me, "I used to get all worried when I went to the grocery store and saw those newspapers by the cash register that say that the world is going to end. You know which ones I mean?"

"Yes."

"Well, now they're not going to worry me anymore, because I can finally prove that what they say isn't true."

"You can?" I asked. "How?"

"Today in the store there was one with a headline that said the world is going to end on October third. Another headline on the same paper said that an asteroid is going to hit the earth on October thirty-first. Then there was another story that said that there is going to be another Great Depression next January. Now, if the world ends on October third, then how could an asteroid hit us on October thirty-first? And if the world has already ended, then how could there be a Great Depression? I don't even know what a Great Depression is, but whatever it is, how could there be one if there's no world anymore?"

"That's good thinking," I said, laughing. "I would never have thought of that, but you're absolutely right; those things *can't* all be true."

"What do you think about ghosts and angels?" he asked, abruptly switching subjects.

Pouring my tea, I lifted the steaming cup into the air. "Have you ever seen a ghost?" Smoky wisps of white steam danced above the cup.

"No," he said. "I've seen angels, but I've never seen any ghosts."

"Do you still remember that?" I asked in wonderment, referring to an episode with angels. "That was a long time ago."

"Yes, I do remember it," he said. "I'll always remember it."

"So will I."

I'll never forget the events of that extraordinary night about six years earlier. Christopher was only three or four years old at the time. His mother and I had awakened at about two o'clock in the morning to the sounds of laughter coming down the hall from Christopher's bedroom. Chris has always slept very soundly, so this was something quite unusual. Sharra got up and went to his room to see what was going on. No more than five minutes later, she reappeared in our bedroom saying, "I think you need to go check this out. I have no idea what is going on. He's seeing things. I felt his forehead, but he doesn't feel feverish at all."

I got out of bed and followed the sound of the laughter. As I came closer to his bedroom, I could make out the sound of talking interspersed with the laughter: "Come here . . . No, you come over here . . ." followed by more giggling. As he saw me walk through his bedroom door, Christopher immediately said, "Daddy! Get that one! The one by your head! Get it! Quick!" The only light in the room came from a small night-light plugged into one of the wall outlets. I looked from side to side, but couldn't see anything near me. Christopher was standing up in his bed, his eyes wide open and darting around the room, his whole face aglow with the most astounding radiance of inno-cent joy I have ever seen. I walked in and sat next to him on the bed. His two little arms were stretched out in front of him, his hands trying to grasp at what appeared to be thin air.

"What are you doing?" I asked him.

"Daddy, don't you see them?" he asked, his attention never leaving the mysterious and, to me, invisible flurry of activity swirling around him.

"See what?" I asked, peering intently into the darkness where I saw his eyes focused.

"Catch one!" he said to me. "Catch that blue one when it comes close to you again!"

I felt his forehead; cool as a cucumber. "Christopher," I said, "Why don't you tell me what to look for. Tell me what you are seeing, and then maybe I can see it, too."

"There are lots of them. Don't you see them?" he said, still reaching out to try to catch them. "They're all different colors: red, blue, green, yellow . . ."

"What are they doing?" I asked him.

"They are flying all around the room, and they want to play with me. They keep telling me to come over there and play with them," he said, pointing to the other side of the room, "but I want them to come over here, 'cause if I get out of my bed, my feet will get cold. Daddy, can you tell more of them to come over here?"

"Do they talk to you?" I asked.

"Of course they do, Daddy. Just listen to them," he said.

"I can't hear them," I admitted, straining my ears anyway. "What do they say?"

"They say they came to play with me," he said, just before erupting with laughter again and lunging in front of my face, his hand grasping at the air again. "Try to get them when they come close to you," he instructed me again.

126

"Who are they?" I asked.

"I don't know, but God sent them," he answered. "Look how small they are!"

I sat there and watched him for a while; I don't remember how long. The intensity of his interest in this strange phenomenon showed no signs of abating even long after he would have lost interest in his favorite toy. His alertness, his eye movements and attempts to reach out and catch these colorful flying spirits convinced me that he truly was seeing something that was not just a figment of his imagination. I felt blessed as I sat there, privileged to be witnessing a sacred encounter, only one side of which I could actually experience. I had seen several angels over the years in sporadic visions, always at unexpected moments, totally beyond my control. The beings I had seen, graceful beyond words, had all been much larger in size than those Christopher was describing to me, were usually solitary in number, and had never spoken to me. How I wished that I could see through his eyes and hear through his ears, if only for a moment. After what may have been a half-hour of my sitting with him on his bed, Christopher fully engaged with his celestial playmates the entire time, his mother appeared at the door, looked hesitantly around the room first, then whispered, "We have *got* to get some sleep tonight." I was in agreement with her about our need for sleep, but was at a complete loss as to how to stop it all.

"Can you tell them good night now?" I asked my son.

"No, Daddy," he said, laughing at my inability to comprehend the situation. "They want to play."

"Well," I said, feeling somewhat guilty at wanting to shut down such a heavenly play-group, "maybe they can keep playing in here while you come and sleep in Mommy and Daddy's bed."

"No, I want to stay here with them," he said.

"I know," I said as I lifted him into my arms, "but it's very late, and we all need to sleep. Maybe they can come back another time and play."

I carried him down the hall then and into the master bedroom. Putting him in the middle between his mother and myself, we both said good night to him and closed our eyes to finally get some sleep. He lay there quietly for a few minutes, long enough that I had just drifted off to sleep once again, when suddenly he sat straight up in bed, laughing his head off. I was jolted back to consciousness with the same unpleasant surge of adrenaline that kicks you awake when the telephone rings in the middle of the night.

"Christopher, what are you doing?" I asked him, putting my arm around him and gently trying to pull him back to the bed that had seemed so peaceful just moments before.

"They're here!" he shouted with delight. "They came to play in here now! Oh, Daddy, look at them all!"

"Oh, no," came a muffled groan from across the bed. "Jeffrey, do something," Sharra said, in a voice that sounded as though it was coming from underneath her pillow.

Meanwhile, Christopher was right back into it. His unseen playmates had followed him to our bedroom, and he was standing on the bed now, laughing, his eyes wide open and darting swiftly here and there around the room, arms reaching out periodically to attempt a catch. I searched the darkness, convinced by some strange logic that I ought to be able to see them now that they were in my own room, but I still could not perceive anything but darkness.

After a few minutes, I sat Christopher down on the bed, his back against the headboard, and asked him to be very quiet so that we could sleep. He seemed to think that would work out all right. I buried my head under my pillow, but

129

before falling asleep again, I could hear the muffled sounds of Christopher laughing somewhere up above me.

In the morning, I asked him if he remembered the events of the previous night, and Christopher readily acknowledged that he did. When I asked him what had happened after his mother and I had finally fallen asleep with him in our bed, he just said that they played for a little bit, but then they had to go, so they left.

"Will they come play with me again?"

I remember hoping that, if they did, it would be during daylight hours, although I wondered if they could only be seen in the dark.

They did not return to play. I asked Christopher frequently over the next couple of months whether he had seen them again, and he said no each time with a voice filled with disappointment. "Are they *ever* going to come and play with me again?" he asked me after another month or two had passed, and I told him I did not know. But I also told him that he must be a very special person to have been visited even once by playmates sent by God. "I know," he said right away. "They told me I was special."

"So you've seen angels," I said to him as he began to sip his now warm Chinese tea, "but you've never seen a ghost."

"No," he said, his eyes widening. "Have you?"

"No, I haven't ever seen a ghost," I said. "But lots of people say they have, don't they?"

"Yes," he said. "What are ghosts?"

"What are they?"

"Yeah. What do you think they really are? Are they really dead people that have come back?"

"The folks who seem to know something about them usually say that ghosts are people who haven't left yet," I said.

"Haven't left yet?"

"Yes," I said. "Some people are so attached to things here on earth, to the house they lived in, or the books they wrote, or the pictures they painted, or even to their families, that they just do not want to leave when they die. So they hang around whatever it is they can't bear to leave behind. It's really pretty sad if it's true, because you have to move on to the next thing that God has in store for you if you want to keep growing."

"So ghosts don't grow anymore?" Chris asked.

"Not as long as they hang around all the stuff that is in their past. But eventually most of them move on to what's next," I assured him. "I don't think that God lets anyone sit around and stop growing for too long, anymore than your mom or I would let you not go to school."

131

"I wish I could know for sure that God is really there," Christopher said at that moment.

"You do know. You've seen angels."

"I know, but those were angels, not God. I want to see God."

"Our cottage is a little distance from here, but how do you know for sure that it's there?" I asked.

"Because I've *seen* it," he countered firmly.

"I don't think that anybody has ever seen God," I said. "I'm not sure that God is something that *can* be seen, so you are probably out of luck there. But you can *feel* God; you can sense that God is there."

"How?" he asked me.

"Because sometimes God just reaches out and grabs you!" I said, reaching under the table and grabbing one of his legs. I started pulling him under the table. Christopher laughed then, and some of his egg drop soup came right out of his nose; I didn't know he had a mouthful, or I would have waited for him to swallow. "Who is pulling your leg, Christopher?" I asked him, as he struggled to keep his dripping chin above the edge of the table.

"You are," he said, giggling and looking furtively around to see if others in the restaurant were watching.

"How do you know it is me?" I asked him, pulling him farther so that all I could see were his eyes looking at me over the table edge, and the ends of his desperately clutching fingers.

"I can see you."

"You can see my arm pulling your leg?" I asked. "All you can see is me sitting way over here on the other side of the table. How do you know that it is my hand holding your leg?"

"It *has* to be yours," he said, making a failing effort not to laugh. "You're the only one it *could* be."

"Right," I said, releasing him. He pulled himself back up into his seat, found his napkin, and wiped the soup off his face. "Christopher," I said, "I just did that to show you two very important things."

"What are they?" he asked attentively.

"First of all, there are times in our lives when God reaches out and grabs hold of us. Usually it is as much of a surprise as when I just grabbed you. If you are paying attention when it happens, you will know that it is God in the same way that you just knew it was me: You just know that God is the only one it could be. There is simply no better explanation."

"What's the second thing?" he asked.

133

"The second thing is that you look pretty silly with egg drop soup coming out of your nose. I wouldn't do that again in public if I were you." We ate the rest of our meal in a much more respectable manner.

O Lord,

support us all the day long,

until the shadows lengthen,

and the evening comes,

and the busy world is hushed,

and the fever of life is over,

and our work is done.

Then in thy mercy,

grant us a safe lodging,

a holy rest,

and peace at the last.

Amen.

—Anglican prayer

EIGHT

Rain visits our lake in different ways. It can come gently and intermittently throughout an entire gray day, timid showers that sprinkle like a whole troupe of dancers upon the water who often falter, then start again, only to retreat hesitantly before attempting their delicate choreography once more. Or it can burst upon us suddenly, a deluge of biblical proportions that drowns out the sight or sound of anything but the tyranny of its own drenching self-importance. It is by far the sudden deluge that is the most eagerly awaited in our family.

When the clouds sweep in from the south, and the sky becomes dark, and the wind dies down to hardly a whisper, we know it is near, and we silently gather on our screened-in porch, one by one, gazing intently down the length of the lake to the south. There is an unspoken rivalry to being the first one to say, "Here it comes!" when "it" at first is nothing more than a vague distortion of our view of the southern shore. But "it" soon draws closer and becomes distinguishable about halfway across the lake, at that range clarifying itself as a massive wall of rain, the front edge of the storm, visually obliterating all that lies behind it and turning the lake beneath into a frothing mass of white water.

Observing the approach of the onslaught is a truly remarkable experience. When such a downpour hits the roof of our little lake house, the noise is not unlike four or five kettledrums being played at the same time and without ceasing. Any meaningful verbal communication must be shouted out to be heard over the din of the rain, so it becomes a perfect opportunity to curl up with a good book, work on a jigsaw puzzle, or just take a nap.

One such torrent had droned its way through the afternoon and into the evening, not letting up until about bedtime. As the noise of the drums subsided up on the roof, it was gradually replaced by the random staccato of drips falling from the leaves overhead, one of nature's most potent sleeping potions. Claire and William had fallen asleep in their beds as they lay reading, surrendering to the hypnotic natural lullaby. I sat on my bed, reading, while Christopher sat at the foot of the bed playing solitaire. Matthew lay on the dog's bed down on the floor, patting Shiva, our greyhound.

"What is it really like when you die?" Christopher asked, breaking the silence.

"What do you mean?" I asked him.

"I mean, is it really like what you see in the movies, with people screaming and blood gushing out of their mouths and ears and everything like that?"

"No, no," I said. "It's hardly ever like that."

"Have you ever seen somebody die?"

"Yes; part of my job is to be with people and their families when they die," I told him.

"How many people have you really been with when they died?" he asked me. "I don't mean that you saw them after they died, but how many have you actually been with while they died?"

"Over the years, probably forty or fifty."

"Wow; what is it like?"

"Well, there are some people who die suddenly in car crashes or some other kind of accident, but for most people death comes when they are very old or because they are very sick, and then it's quite peaceful, just like falling asleep."

"My friend John's grandfather just died," Chris said through a huge yawn. "He was really nice, and I liked him a lot. He lived in their house with them, and I always saw him when I went over to play with John. The day he died, he was fine. He had lunch with them, and then he went to his room to take a nap. He never woke up; he just died while he was sleeping."

"That's how it happens for most people," I said. "Whether they're old or just really sick, usually they fall asleep, and then pass away while they are sleeping."

"John saw his grandfather after he had died. He said he looked pretty much the same, except he was really pale and white."

"Yes," I said. "People don't usually look very different when they die, just a little paler."

"Dad, I don't need to be afraid of going to sleep, do I? I mean, that's not going to happen to me, right? I'm not going to just not wake up sometime, am I?"

"Christopher," I chuckled, "you are never going to not wake up, even when you die. It's just that when you die, the people you leave here don't see you when you wake up that time, because you're waking up in a whole different place."

"A good place, I hope," he said through another yawn, putting aside his deck of cards and lying back on the bed. "But I still wonder what it's like when that happens."

"I heard a wonderful story once, a story about what it must be like when we die," I told him.

"Can you tell us?" came Matthew's voice from somewhere below the bed. "I would like to hear it."

"Me, too," Christopher said, fighting to keep his eyes open.

"Okay," I said. "But then you have to go to bed, because it's getting late."

"Okay."

"In this story, life is a lot like a day at the beach," I began. "One summer day, a little boy went to the beach with his mom and dad. It was a bright, warm, sunny day, and the boy was so excited because he *loved* the beach. He brought his bathing suit and big beach towel, his pail and shovel, his Frisbee, his brand-new kite, and his air mattress. When they arrived at the beach, the boy didn't know what he wanted to do first, so he just ran down to the water, threw some rocks out into the ocean as far as he could, and he ran down the beach after the gulls and sandpipers, making them scamper and fly off in all directions. The tide was out pretty far now, so he decided to build a big sand castle, one with a huge wall around it to protect it from the waves when the tide came back in. He worked hard, digging and piling and shaping the sand until finally his castle was finished, its towers standing tall and the wall around its deep moat thick and strong.

"Once the castle was built, he realized that the tide had turned and was beginning to come back in. He raced down the beach with his pail, looking for the most beautiful seashells before they were covered by the incoming surf. He found lots of shells, and his pail was full of them when he finally walked back to his parents. By then it was lunchtime, so he sat on his big beach towel and ate the sandwich his mother had made him, along with some potato chips and a pickle. For dessert he had three big chocolate chip cookies and finished two glasses of pink lemonade.

"There was a good strong breeze coming in off the ocean, so after lunch his father asked him if he wanted to fly his new kite. They took it out of its package and his dad put it together for him. It was a large box kite, and when they tossed it up into the wind, it climbed and climbed so far that before long it was just a little dot against the blue of the sky. They tied the string to a rock on the beach after a while, so that the boy could bury his father in the sand. They dug and dug the biggest hole they could until it was big enough for Dad, who lay down in it and let the boy fill it all in, until only his dad's head was sticking up out of the sand. He ran and got his mother, who came over and laughed at what they had done, and then quickly started reeling in the kite, because it had begun to drop as the breeze died down. Once the kite was back on the ground and secure, the boy and his mother threw the Frisbee to each other along the beach for a long time.

"The waves of the incoming surf were a little bigger now, since the tide was coming back in, so the boy dug his dad out of the sand and asked him to blow up his air mattress for him. He paddled on the mattress out a little ways into the water, and rode the waves back in toward shore. It was so much fun. Sometimes he would fall off the mattress into the surf and sand, but his dad would pull him right back up and put him on the mattress again, so he wasn't scared. It was on one of those rides that he suddenly noticed his sand castle was surrounded by water, and the surf was slowly eroding the wall

 that protected the castle. He ran over and began rebuilding the wall with more sand. But as the tide came in, the waves hitting the wall got bigger and bigger, until finally they swept over the outer wall and reached the castle. The castle

slowly melted down until it was nothing more than a little lump on the flat wet sand.

"It was then that the boy began to realize how tired he was. He looked up and saw that the sun was low on the horizon; many other people had already left the beach. His shoulders and face had begun to hurt; he was red with sunburn. He was covered with sand from head to toe, and the sand was in his ears and on his lips and in his eyes. His ankles itched with bites from sand fleas, and his knees and elbows were red and sore; they had been scraped by the sand when he had fallen off his air mattress riding the waves. For the first time that whole day, the boy couldn't think of anything else he wanted to do. He was so tired, and he just wanted to rest. He walked back up to his big beach towel, and he lay down on it and closed his eyes, hearing the roar of the surf behind him, clutching the softness of the towel beneath him, and feeling the cool ocean breeze caressing his sunburned back. He thought of all the things he had done that day on the beach, and he smiled. Before long, he was fast asleep.

"The very next thing that little boy was aware of was that he rolled over, but instead of feeling his towel beneath him, he felt the cool, clean sheets of his own bed. Instead of his bathing suit, he was wearing his pajamas. Instead of feeling the sand grating against his sunburned skin, he realized that he was clean, and his skin was soft and smooth because someone had rubbed lotion all over his sunburn. He opened his eyes, and saw that it was a new morning, and that he was waking up in his own bedroom at home, clean and comfortable, but he didn't even remember how he had come to be there.

"That is exactly what I think it is like when we die," I said.

Matthew said, "Cool," from below the bed, but Christopher was silent. Looking down the bed, I could see that his eyes were closed and his mouth was wide open. I prodded him with my foot; no response. I called out his name; no response. Finally, I stood up, picked him up into my arms, and carried him to his bed, where he nestled down under the covers without even waking up.

The next morning, emerging from his room, Christopher approached me with a sheepish grin on his face. "How did I get to my bed last night?" he asked.

"You don't remember?"

"No, I don't."

"What do you remember?" I asked.

"Just that story you were telling me about some boy on a beach, but I don't remember anything after he was flying that kite. And I don't remember going to my bed."

"That's what it's like," I said.

"That's what *what* is like?" he asked.

"Dying. And waking up in heaven. And not remembering how we got there."

"Oh," he said. And after a long reflective pause, he smiled and said, "Oh, yeah . . . that's what I was asking you about, wasn't it? You really think it's like that? That would be awesome, wouldn't it, if that were really true?"

"Awesome," I agreed. "Want to hear the rest of the story after they flew the kite?" But he was already on his way out the front door. The rain was over, the sun was shining, and my son was determined to make the most of another new day at the lake.

Where can I go then from your Spirit?

Where can I flee from your presence?

If I climb up to heaven, you are

there; if I make the grave my bed,

you are there also.

If I take the wings of the morning

and dwell in the uttermost parts

of the sea,

Even there your hand will lead

me and your right hand hold me fast.

If I say, "Surely the darkness

will cover me,

and the light around me turn to night,"

Darkness is not dark to you;

the night is as bright as the day;

darkness and light to you are

both alike.

—Psalm 139

NINE

Each summer, there is perhaps one night in which the lake takes on a totally different character, absolutely mythical in its appearance. Several factors must interact in just the right way for this to happen, and a few days after our unexpectedly long trip to the grocery store, they did.

At about ten-thirty one night, the accustomed breeze coming in from the lake had died down to nothing. The air was perfectly still; not the slightest quiver could be seen in the leaves of the trees or the grass below. Absent the constant sound of the wind in the trees, there was little sound at all: an occasional voice from across the lake, the intermittent croaking of a bullfrog, and, piercing the silence at regular intervals, the other-worldly cries of loons calling to one another in the darkness. Overhead, the night sky had finally emptied itself of the light that lingered in the western quadrant for over an hour after the setting of the sun. With that departure the stars had taken hold of the sky, sweeping over the whole vault of the heavens and transforming it into a dazzling canopy of diamonds, their brilliant light amplified by the stark blackness in which they were set. Not the merest wisp of cloud rode the evening sky that night. The moon was but a thin sliver of itself, enabling the full splendor of this celestial symphony to bathe the earth with the fullness of its breathtaking beauty. So brightly did the stars shine that to look up at them, one had to squint at first to shield one's eyes from their stabbing fire. So still was the air that the surface of the lake was a sheet of mirrored glass, reflecting every star so perfectly that to gaze into it was to gaze into another sky. In fact, standing on the edge of the lake that night invited the clear illusion that one was standing at the edge of a vortex, a cosmic doorway the size of our lake leading to a parallel universe that stretched out, infinite, below.

It was into that profound fantasy that our boat made its way, slowly so as not to disturb the water, gently easing down the anchor once we had reached the middle. Our voices did not rise above the softest whisper, so struck with awe were our minds and our souls. Our boat had become a vehicle capable of interstellar flight that night, silently floating through the universe, inter-galactic space stretching out both above and below us wherever we looked. Matthew, Claire, Christopher, and I, reclining the chairs in the boat, lay on our backs looking straight up. After a few minutes the Russian space station *Mir* passed by, much brighter than the other satellites we saw. We spoke of how much brighter the new international space station was going to be once it was completed. A shooting star singed its dying light across the sky, and then another.

"What are those?" Christopher asked.

"Meteorites," I answered.

"How big are they?" Christopher softly asked the universe, his voice seeming to echo faintly through the entire cosmos in the silence.

"Not very big anymore," came a whisper and a giggle from Claire.

"I mean how big do they have to be to explode on the earth, like in *Deep Impact* or *Armageddon*?" Chris asked.

"*Deep Impact* is about a comet, not a meteorite," Matthew whispered in clarification, "and *Armageddon* is about an asteroid."

"I *know* that, Matthew," Chris said in a frustrated but low voice that he quickly modified down into a whisper. "But I just want to know how big something has to be to get through the atmosphere, and how many of them are out there, and whether any of them are actually coming toward us."

"Those shooting stars are meteorites that are not very big at all," I said. "To make it all the way down to the surface of the earth, it has to be a pretty-good-sized chunk of rock, because so much of it is going to burn up in the atmosphere."

"How often does that happen?" Chris asked.

"As I understand it, it happens quite often—every day, in fact. But the size of the meteorites once they hit the surface is so small that they don't do much damage," I said. "Our atmosphere protects us very, very well."

"But it can't protect us from a really big asteroid," Chris said.

"No," I agreed, "but those don't come along very often."

"One like that killed all the dinosaurs," Claire said.

Matthew quickly added, "And in the early 1900s, a big one hit Siberia and knocked down all the trees for miles. I saw pictures of it once."

"Dad," Christopher said, "I have a friend at school who says that the world is going to end in the year 2000. Do you think that's true?"

"No, I don't," I answered.

"But he says that the Bible even tells us that it is going to happen," he continued, "back in the last book of the Bible."

"Revelation?"

"Yes. I couldn't remember the name."

"The person who wrote Revelation," I said, "was part of a community that was being persecuted because they were Christians. They were sure that their lives were going to come to an end soon. Their world was going to end, and the last book of the Bible is something a man named John wrote to try to give some meaning to what they were going through, and to give them the hope that, even if they all lost their lives, everything would still be okay because God would be in control of all of it."

"If they all got killed, everything would still be okay," Christopher echoed, double-checking to see if I actually meant to say something so ridiculous.

"Yes," I said.

"And if a giant asteroid came and destroyed the earth, I mean blew it apart so there was no earth anymore, like some people say is going to happen soon, everything would still be okay?" he probed further.

"Yes."

"Yes?"

"Yes."

Then, after a pause, "How can it be *yes*?" Christopher asked incredulously. He sat up suddenly, tipping the boat, and sending out a series of shock waves so powerful that they completely distorted our view of the universe below us as they plowed through it.

"Heyyyy . . . stop moving," his brother and sister moaned softly in protest, both now enthralled with the mirrored cosmos in the water. Chris lay down again, slowly.

I stretched my arms up and opened my hands so that, from my own perspective at least, it appeared that I could have gathered all the stars that lay between them and squeezed them together, like a snowball, into one large ball of pure light. "You know that song 'He's Got the Whole World in His Hands'?" I asked.

"Yeah," Christopher said sarcastically, "unless the whole world is blown to bits."

"I think God is much larger than that; I think

God has the whole universe in his hands," I said. "And you are much larger than you think you are, too, Christopher; you are a child of the God of the whole universe, and with God looking out for you, there is nothing in this universe that can ever really hurt you."

"Unless my whole planet is destroyed," he murmured.

"In the book of Revelation," I said, "Saint John says that even if the world comes to an end, it will turn out to be the beginning of a whole new age, with God still in control of it all. The most important belief we have as Christians is that on the other side of any kind of death there is always newer, greater life. Always. That's what Jesus was trying to show us with his resurrection."

"Do you *want* the world to end?" Christopher asked me, with the accusatory tone of a prosecuting attorney.

"Of course I don't want the world to end," I answered. "I don't know of *anybody* who would want the world to end. And I don't think that an asteroid is going to blow us to bits anytime soon, by the way. You just asked me about the book of Revelation, and in that book John is trying to comfort a bunch of scared people who know that they are probably about to be arrested and killed by telling them that even if the entire world were to end, God would make sure they were all okay. You've been telling me how scared you are of dying, and what I'm trying to tell you is that whether you die in your sleep when you are a hundred and two years old, or a giant asteroid comes out of nowhere tonight and blows the whole earth apart, you are going to be okay, because God will make sure that you are. Believing that is true, no matter what can ever possibly happen, is called faith."

"But how can I know that God is there?" he asked me.

"There are different ways of knowing different kinds of things," I said. "Some things can be seen, like these stars; and some very real things can't be seen, like God. And the confusing part is that a lot of things that we can see aren't what we think they are—they are illusions; but some of the things that we *can't* see turn out to be more important and more real than a lot of things that we *can* see. Christopher, as you go through this life, you are going to run into a lot of shadows and illusions along the way, and one of the most important skills you need to learn as early as possible is how to tell the difference between what is real and what is just an illusion. Do you know what an illusion is?"

"It's something that looks different from what it really is?" he said.

"Right," I said. "Have you ever looked at the road way up ahead of the car on a really hot day?"

"Oh, yeah. It looks like water."

"So what if you kept slowing your car down every time you saw that, because you thought there was a huge puddle in the road ahead?"

"You wouldn't ever get to where you were going," he said, chuckling.

"Well, you'd probably get there eventually, but it sure would take you a lot longer than it should have," I said. "And it's the same way in life. You simply won't grow and learn as fast as God wants you to if you are living your life and basing your decisions on illusions and shadows instead of those things that are real."

"What do you mean?" he asked.

"I can show you an example right now," I said. "Let's say that you are the captain of the starship *Enterprise*, and you want to go to that galaxy right there, that bright one in the middle of the handle of the Big Dipper. Do you see it?"

"Yes," he said.

"You're going to head out there at warp speed, so you have to program in your direction

161

before you go to warp speed. Which direction are you going to go?" I asked.

"I'm going to go toward the galaxy."

"It *looks* as though you should just aim your ship at that particular spot in the sky and go for it, doesn't it? But the fact is that if you did that, you would probably end up a good distance from where that galaxy really is."

"I would?" Christopher said. "Why?"

"Because most of the stars in the sky are not really where we see them; their light has been bent around other objects, such as huge stars and black holes, which have a lot of gravity. In fact, as we look up, we actually see the images of some stars in two or three different places in the sky at once, because the light from those stars has been bent in a couple of directions as it makes its way to earth. So if we aimed our ship for where we can *see* the star, we would miss it; it turns out that most of what we can see of the universe around us is an illusion. But the gravity that causes the illusion is real, and gravity is something we can't even see. Have you ever heard that expression, 'Things are not always as they appear to be'?"

"Yes," he said thoughtfully; then continued in a voice that had just a tinge of anxiety, as if he were afraid that the integrity of the very fabric of reality itself was in danger of coming loose around him, "What other illusions are there that I should know about?"

"Well, you told me you wanted to see God. Do you see him anywhere out there?" I asked him.

"No."

"There's another illusion, because God is everywhere; he fills the entire universe, like gravity, but you can't even see him, and that is a dangerous illusion to mistake for reality, because you will wind up living your life thinking that you're all alone, when you are actually resting right in the arms of God the whole time, and you will decide that too many wonderful things in this world happen simply because they happen that way, without realizing each time that it is only the hand of God that could have made it so."

"But you can't prove that God is there. At least you can prove that gravity is real."

"We can? Do you know that there is not one scientist in the world who understands why there is gravity? They think there might be a really small particle called a graviton that makes gravity work, but so far no one has ever been able to find one of those. Truth is, not one single person knows what gravity is or how it works. But we all believe in gravity anyway, don't we? Scientists have faith in the force of gravity, even though they can't see it or prove how it works at all."

"But gravity is *real*," he said emphatically. "You can *feel* it."

"The same guy who wrote that last book in the Bible also wrote a gospel and some letters that are in the New Testament, too," I told him. "In one of the letters, he says that God is love. Is love something that is real, Christopher?"

"Yes," he said immediately.

"Can you prove that love really exists?" I asked.

"People love each other," he said. "Everybody loves somebody; everybody knows that love exists."

"Do you love me?"

"Yes."

"Can you prove to me that you love me?"

There was a long silence, punctuated by the long, plaintive cry of a loon from the other side of the lake and by the sound of Claire's teeth chattering with the chill of another Maine night setting in; she had not brought her sweater with her.

"No," said Chris, "I can't. But I do love you; you know that I do."

"I know that you love me, and you know that I love you, and neither one of us can prove it, can we, to each other or to anybody else?" I said.

"It's a different way of knowing, to know things that can't be seen. Saint John says that the love you feel is God—not just a part of what God is, like a color or a shape, but the whole of what God is; God is love itself. Now, according to John, you *do* know that God is real, because you know that love is real. That's one of the reasons that you have to be part of some kind of community, living close to other people in order to be close to God. God can grab hold of us out of the blue, when we stand in the presence of his overwhelming majesty as we do under these stars tonight, or he can grab us through another person, another person that we truly love."

"How does he do that?" Chris asked.

"God is love. When I feel my love for you, I'm feeling God alive inside of me. When I see you loving me, I'm seeing God alive inside of you. It works both ways, and that love that we feel is more real than just about anything else we know, isn't it?"

Claire came over just then and put her arms around me silently, hugging me tightly. I hugged her back, thinking of how lucky we all were to share so much love, to know so much of God in that way. That sentiment was only partially dampened by the sound of chattering teeth and her voice whispering in my ear that she was just trying to warm up, and if we could please go home now.

Christopher, meanwhile, was sitting and gazing up at the sky. His hands, open in front of him, were moving up and down just the slightest bit, as if in supplication. His mouth was open as if ready to utter something profound, but the only sound to emerge was, "Dad . . ."

"Yes?"

"I can't say what I'm feeling. I don't know the right words," he stammered, worlds of frustration within his voice.

"Are you feeling something good?" I asked.

"Yes . . . it's . . . awesome . . . it's . . . I don't know how to say it," came the response, his face still looking up, as if the right words should appear for him in the heavens. I reached over in the darkness and gently took hold of his leg.

"It's okay, Christopher," I said quietly. "Maybe there aren't any words; maybe God is grabbing you."

We rode back to our dock without discussion, each with our own thoughts. I had the distinct sense that my son had been touched that night. I had been touched in the same way over the years, yet I did not speak to him of it again. Some secrets of the night are imparted silently and should remain that way.

Yea, though I walk through the

valley of the shadow of death,

I will fear no evil;

for thou art with me;

thy rod and thy staff, they comfort me.

—Psalm 23

TEN

Bass fishing has become a competitive family enterprise in recent years, starting when my son Matthew landed an eighteen-and-a-half-inch smallmouth during the summer of 1994. It hangs mounted above the fireplace, a standard that has since taunted every person heading out on the lake to fish.

Early summer is always witness to a new expedition to the local outfitter in the hope that over the winter somebody has developed the most irresistible lure yet for big, fat, hungry bass scouting out their next meal. Fishing poles are reassembled; reels are adjusted to just the right drag and loaded with line that will withstand even the most valiant fighter; and tackle boxes are loaded with magic worms, salamanders, slugs, minnows, and crayfish that float and dive and wiggle and swim—all made of plastic and dripping with sharp hooks that point their menacing fangs in every direction. Each lure is designed to seduce even the most experienced, wary bass into thinking that it is looking at the most delicious, satisfying tidbit it has ever come across. Thus armed, the intrepid warriors are off to do battle, lying in wait for their chance to pull in "the big one," the fish so large that all others will seem minuscule by comparison.

The biggest fish seem to bite most readily in the first light of morning, so that is when my young fishermen go forth, pulling themselves from their beds at about five o'clock, bundling themselves against the chill, tossing a pop-tart into their tackle boxes, and paddling into the mist that shrouds the lake like a soft white blanket until the sun burns it away. On successful mornings, there is satisfaction enough for all, because while my boys love to fish, they do not enjoy eating fish. On the other hand, Claire and I love nothing more than fresh, sweet bass or white perch for breakfast, but we do not enjoy the early rising, nor the battle with bugs, damp, and cold that go with those early hours. And the timing is perfect: by the time Claire and I are rising and thinking about breakfast, the fishermen have usually returned.

It was on one such morning that Christopher broke his own personal record, landing a smallmouth that measured a full eighteen inches in length, two-and-a-half inches longer than his previous best and almost as large as the behemoth of Matthew's that swims the air above the mantle. The first news of it came from William, running up the path that winds its way from the dock to the cottage, shouting "Dad! . . . Dad! . . . Dad!" repeatedly. By the time I arrived at the dock, the fish was laid out on the cutting board, the subject of a detailed forensic dissection by Matthew before its final cleaning and scaling. Its stomach was huge and, when opened, revealed three entire crayfish, causing me to wonder how it could have possibly swallowed another, the lure having been a fairly good facsimile. Christopher, not yet old enough to wield the sharp knife for cleaning fish, observed the proceedings from the sidelines.

As Matthew began to scale the fish, Christopher said, "Dad, do fish have souls?" and I chuckled as I heard the question, because it reminded me so much of a similar question that had been put to Thomas Aquinas about eight hundred years ago, as to whether dogs and women had souls. Aquinas wrestled with the inquiry throughout several pages of his *Summa Theologica*, and finally concluded that no, dogs do not have souls, and then stated that he just couldn't be sure about women.

"I think that every living creature has a soul," I said to him, bucking against old Tom.

"Crayfish, too?" he asked.

"Even crayfish."

"Will this fish and these crayfish go to heaven, then?"

"Maybe not to the same kind of heaven that people enjoy," I answered. "But life doesn't ever end, so I'm sure that God has a very special plan for creatures like this when they die. They continue to grow, too."

It was my grandmother who taught me that fish that are truly fresh have no odor. Every Friday a fish truck would pass through the streets of her little town of Dresden, Maine, laden with fresh seafood from the coast. The man who drove the truck would come to her front door and ask if she wanted some fish that day. My grandmother would usually ask him if he had hake or halibut. With most customers, he would simply return to the door in a couple of minutes with whatever measure of scallops, salmon, halibut, hake, mackerel, etc. had been requested, wrapped up nicely in white butcher's paper. To the fishmonger's dismay, my grandmother always insisted on walking out to his truck and personally subjecting the catch to her rigorous smell test, rejecting any that had the slightest "fishy" odor to it. She was very much on my mind when, less than an hour after being caught, Christopher's odor-free bass was placed in the frying pan. It made a sumptuous breakfast for Claire and me.

Later that afternoon Chris and I took the dog for a walk around the island. I complimented him on his astounding catch that morning, and he regaled me with a detailed account of how it all had happened. When we were done with that subject, he launched into another topic that was concerning him:

"Dad, is our religion the right one?" I couldn't help but observe with deep satisfaction that his questions had recently taken on a different quality; whereas his earlier enquiries had questioned the very existence of God, the majority of them lately held within them the assumption that God was real.

"I think that most of the major religions are right about a lot of things," I said. "But remember that big jigsaw puzzle that forms a picture of the total truth about God? The different religions of the world are like different people standing around a table, trying to piece together the whole picture of truth. Each religion has a bunch of the pieces, and tries to imagine what the finished picture looks like just from looking at their own little group of pieces. But nobody has the complete picture, and the sad thing is that we have always seemed to fight about the parts of the larger picture that just aren't in place yet; we argue about the things that we don't know and

175

can't see, instead of sharing and celebrating the parts that we do know about."

"What are the things that we all know about?" Chris asked.

"For thousands of years now," I told him, hoping that I wasn't leading him into water that was over his head, "the different religions of this world have been stewards of a great and mysterious truth; they have, each in their own special way, held up for people the wisdom that there is far more to reality than most of us can see or touch or detect at all with our five senses. The details of what that greater reality consists of and how it all works, whether it is heaven or hell or angels or even God, are a little different from one religion to another, because most of those details are not clear to any of us; they are the missing pieces of that big puzzle that people have argued about so often. But we all believe that there is more to reality than we can normally see, and we all believe that there is a divine being of great love and goodness that we call God, who created and who continues to manage the whole universe—the parts we can see and the parts we can't. And it is for that reason that Jesus, as well as spiritual leaders in other traditions, has said things like, 'Judge not . . .' down through the ages. In other words,

Jesus is warning us not to make too many hard and fast judgments about other people, or other religions, or God, or what is fair and unfair in life, simply because we just do not have all the information we really need to make those kinds of judgments. Do you understand what I'm saying so far?"

"I think so," Chris said. "I guess that we could use that old saying 'There's more to this than meets the eye' as the title of this lesson."

My heart soared. "Yes," I said with enthusiasm, the two of us doing a high-five in the middle of the road. "That's a perfect title for what I'm trying to say. But listen to this," I went on, confident now that he could grasp what I was about to tell him, "because this is the really exciting part. In just the past few years, really just since you were born, scientists have discovered that what religions have been saying all these thousands of years is true. Can you imagine science and religion saying the same thing?"

"Really?" he said.

"Really. Scientists called small-particle physicists have been studying matter for years now, examining smaller and smaller pieces of all this 'stuff' that makes up the universe. They've gone from discovering molecules to atoms, and then on to discovering particles that are even smaller than atoms, particles that they can only observe with those huge, circular tubes that are called particle accelerators. Have you ever seen a picture of one of those?"

"Yes," Chris said.

"Well, when they smash some of these subatomic particles together in a special accelerator, called a superconducting supercollider, they can see some amazing things happening. And one of the most amazing things they have seen is that there is a whole lot more to the fabric of reality than any of us can see," I said.

"They have? Have *they* seen angels, too?"

"No, not angels, but a lot more of reality. Now you're going to have to pay close attention, and tell me if you don't understand, okay?"

"Okay."

"We live in four dimensions," I said. "Do you know what different dimensions are?"

"Well," he said, "In *Star Trek*, they sometimes fall into other dimensions, like other universes."

"What I'm talking about is a little different than that," I said. "We spend our lives moving around in four dimensions. Three of them are dimensions having to do with space: height, width, and depth. The fourth one is time; we go forward in time. Are you with me?"

"Yes."

"All most people are aware of are these four dimensions to reality. But scientists now have observed six to eight *other* dimensions, and those are just as real as the four that we see and use. The universe, it turns out, is made up of ten to twelve dimensions. That means that all of us are going through our lives and making decisions based on our awareness of only about a *third* of the fullness of reality that is all around us. That's like giving somebody a photograph of a strawberry and asking him to tell you what it smells like, and how it tastes. In other words, scientists are now telling us the same thing that religions have been telling us for the past five or six thousand years: There is a lot more to all of this than meets the eye."

"What *are* those other dimensions?" Chris asked.

"The scientists don't really know. They can see what effects they have on matter, but they don't know *why* they work that way yet. Even scientists have some pieces missing from *their* big picture puzzle of reality, and they argue with each other about the missing parts, too."

We walked on a little farther, and I could almost hear the wheels turning in Christopher's head. As we walked through the shadowy stretch that bounds the northern end of the island, towering ancient pine trees flanking our path, he suddenly broke the silence.

"I don't understand something."

"What's that?"

"Why won't God let us see all the other parts of reality?"

"I don't know, Christopher; I've had that same question for a while now. The only thing that I keep coming up with is that we're just not ready yet. You know how, when you play most of your video games, you have to beat one level before you can go to the next one, and they get harder as they go?"

"Yeah."

"Well, I figure that it's something like that," I said. "We never ever stop growing and learning, and I think that God makes us learn certain lessons before he lets us go on to the next level. We probably wouldn't be able to handle twelve dimensions the way we are; we have a hard enough time dealing with only four. But maybe when we do well with four, God lets us live with six for a while, and then eight when we master those. We could probably do a lot more damage to this universe with twelve dimensions than we can with four."

"But if there's so much more to all of this than we can see or touch, then how are we supposed to be able to decide anything or to live our lives without messing everything up?" he asked.

"That's an excellent question," I said, "and religions have tried to give people answers over the years. Saint Paul had a good suggestion, in our religion. He said, 'Be of good courage. Hold fast to that which is good. Render to no one evil for evil. Strengthen the fainthearted, support the weak, help and cheer the sick, honor every human being.'"

"That's nice," he said, "but it's mostly about how I treat other people. What about me?"

"Remember the other night when we were talking about the end of the world?" I asked.

"Yes."

"There are only three things in this universe that are *really* real," I said, "things that are still there even if everything else is gone. Those are the things to hold to; those are the things that should guide your decisions in life. I told you that there are many illusions and shadows to watch out for in this life, and it's true. But if you hold on to the things that are real, then you can avoid a lot of mess-ups. What do you think are the three things that are real, that are going to be there no matter what?"

"I bet you're going to say that one of them is God," he said.

181

"I don't have to now, because you just did," I said. "And the other two things are things that only come from God: life and love. Christopher, if you place God at the center of your life, then you will always be strong. If you make every one of your decisions based on what will bring more life to you and to those around you, then you will always be fully alive. And if you love others with an unconditional love, not always trying to get something from people, but loving them no matter what you ever get back, then you will never ever be alone. Things that do not give life, things that do not support love are all illusions; they do not last, and never will. They may look good on the surface, but it's just an illusion; there is nothing to them, and they can't last. One of our most important tasks in this life is to learn to tell the difference between what is real and what is illusion. Life and love are the only two things in this world that will still be there no matter what happens, because life and love both have the substance of God within them; they can *only* come from God. If you constantly guide your life by them, you can never go wrong, and you won't be sucked in by all the illusions and shadows that you encounter along the way."

"What do you mean by shadows?" he asked.

182

"Things that are real cast shadows if there is a bright light on the other side of them, don't they?" I said.

"Yes," he answered.

"And those shadows can be scary, can't they, especially if they are big?"

"Yes; I have one in my bedroom at home that scares me every night."

"A shadow is real in a way; I mean, you can see it, but what is a shadow, really?" I asked.

"Nothing," Chris said.

"Right; it's really nothing at all except a place where the light is blocked. Now, a shadow can only come from something that is real, right? A shadow can't cast another shadow, true?"

"True."

"Okay," I said. "Now think about this, because it's the most important thing that I want you to remember from our discussions this summer. What did we just agree are the only two real, solid, lasting things in this world?"

"Life and love?"

"Yes. Life and love. They both come from God, who is the brightest light there is in the whole universe," I said. "With that kind of light behind them, and because of how real they are, they each cast a very big shadow. And their shadows appear to be the opposite of themselves. Since

183

both life and love are very, very good things, their shadows are very, very scary. Do you know what we call these two shadows?" I asked.

There was another long silence, filled only with the sound of our footsteps on the gravel beneath us.

"What is the shadow of life?" I asked.

"Death?" he asked back.

"Yes," I said. "When God, the purest, brightest light there is, comes close to a person, when it is time for that life to leave its broken body and move on so that it can continue to grow, then a very big, very dark shadow is cast. Sometimes all that we can see is that shadow and an empty body, and we call it death. Now what do you think is the shadow of love?"

"Hate?" he asked.

"No," I said, "but you are close; the shadow of love is fear. People only hate because they fear. God is love. Real, unconditional love is God shining through a person. When we mistakenly assume that love is something that has to flow *from* us to others instead of *through* us, then a huge shadow is cast between us and those around us, because we are not capable of loving anybody in a perfect way on our own, and we know it. If we are not open to God's love flowing through us, then we actually *block* God's love.

God is so close behind each of us that it causes a big, dark shadow right in front of us that we see wherever we go, a shadow that *we* are causing ourselves, because we are not really letting God into our lives.

"Without God in our lives, life will be filled with fear; we will always be wondering who or what is going to get us, and we won't be able to trust anybody or anything. We will always be living in that shadow called fear. On the other hand, if we know that on our own we can't love the way we are supposed to, and we open ourselves up enough to let God's love, real love, flow through us to others, then there will be no shadow; we will not fear anything. When you experience God's love flowing into you and out of you like that, then you know that nothing in this world can ever really hurt you, because God is always there with you, and is always going to be. So fear suddenly disappears the way all shadows eventually do when the light hits them.

"Sometimes we hear Bette Midler singing 'The Rose' on the radio. It's a beautiful song, and one of the lines is, 'It's the soul afraid of dying that never learns to live.' It's true, Christopher; we have a choice in this life to live without God or to live with God, to live our lives in the shadows or to live our lives in the sunlight. God wants us to live with a love for life, not a fear of death. That's why God made us: so that we can know the joy of experiencing his life and his love flowing through us to others, and back to us again. If people spend most of their lives fearing death, and living in that shadow, which is really nothing at all, then it is sad, because they are wasting so much time, when they could be loving with every bit of their lives instead.

"As you go through life, Christopher, be careful not to get caught up in all the illusions that do not give real life or pure love; they're just distractions. And when you find yourself standing in the shadows we call fear and death, try to remember then that those shadows are so dark only because God is so close. Call on God at those times to bring you out of the shadows, and he will; he's always right there, you know, to help you with anything you need, if you will just let him."

We returned to our driveway as I was still speaking, and the three other siblings came clamoring for rides around the lake on the tube. Matthew and Claire walked with me down the well-worn path that winds its way through the massive old pine trees and over the lichen-covered rocks to the dock. William rode high up on my shoulders, patting out the rhythm of our footsteps on my bald head. As the four of us began to remove the canvas from the boat, I looked for Chris, who had not accompanied us, but he was nowhere in sight. Leaving the dock, I walked up through the pine grove to the hammock, where I had a better view of the driveway behind the house. There was Christopher, sitting alone on the swing set. His face was completely devoid of expression, and his eyes were staring off into the woods, unfocused. I could tell his mind was processing something important. I was almost ready to walk back up to him, thinking that perhaps there was unfinished business to be resolved from the discussion we had dropped rather suddenly. Just then Christopher stood up, looked at the ground for a second, as if making a last-minute mental review of some important data, and then leaped into a full run toward the rest of us, his face adorned with a huge smile.

With the boat uncovered and rigged for tubing, Matthew and Claire took their positions on the double tube. William sat facing backward in the spotter's seat, and Chris went to his favorite spot in the bow, his face still holding that grin. Off we went into the lake as we had done a hundred times before, except this time things were qualitatively different. I sensed a lightness in the air around Christopher, as if a pall had been lifted from his countenance. He propped himself up on his knees on the bow cushion, leaning back with the bowline in his hands. The wind swept his hair back over his head. He had not uttered a single word since our conversation on the road, but he turned his head back toward me now and shouted, "Dad! I'm feeling more of myself up here! My soul is rejoicing!" I smiled at him and nodded.

We rounded the other side of the lake and headed straight into the afternoon sun, creating an image that will grace my mind's eye for a long time to come. The sun reflected now on the water in front of us, throwing a thousand tiny brilliant flashes our way; it seemed as though Christopher's little angels had returned to play and were dancing on the waves ahead, leading us toward the sun, splashing light in every direction. From my perspective, Christopher's head eclipsed the sun. His brown hair, standing up in the wind, had taken on a golden aura as the sun's light came through it. He held his arms out like wings, as if to fly, in that moment reminding me of Moses parting the Red Sea and Leonardo DiCaprio riding the snout of the *Titanic*. Then, wafting somewhere above the sound of the wind and the waves and the motor behind us, came another sound, the faint but distinct resonance of Christopher's voice, belting out a song at the top of his lungs to the brilliance of creation dancing in front of him:

This is the life that never ends,

It just goes on and on my friends;

Some people started livin' it not knowin' what it was,

And they'll just keep on livin' it forever, just because . . .

This is the life that never ends,

It just goes on and on my friends;

Some people started livin' it not knowin' what it was,

And they'll just keep on livin' it forever, just because . . .

I started singing with him, and then William joined in. Chris turned when he heard us and smiled at me. Our eyes locked, and my heart was so full that I thought it would burst right through my chest. What a way to go, I remember thinking. I yelled, "I love you!" to him, and he yelled back, "I love you more!" and we returned to our never-ending song of life. Tears welled up in my eyes, tears of pride and profound love; above all else, they were tears of gratitude to the God who made us all. My son had climbed out of the valley of the shadow of death and, at least for the present moment, there was nothing in all creation that could shake him.

We wait in the darkness!

Come, Ye who listens,

Help in our night journey:

Now no sun is shining;

Now no star is glowing;

Come show us the pathway:

The night is not friendly;

The moon has deceived us,

We wait in the darkness!

—Iroquois prayer[7]

ELEVEN

The evening of that same day stood witness to four exhausted children tumbling into their beds. Happy victims of sun, water, wind, and fun, they could hardly keep their eyes open as the hands of the clock completed their final sweep toward the appointed hour.

While I was a young child, I was afraid to go to sleep at night. I thought that I might die during the night and never wake up again. Even when the day had been long and my eyes just would not stay open any longer, I would lie in my bed and fight the demon striving to pull the thick pall of unconsciousness over me. As sleep encroached on my waning awareness and I realized I was fighting a losing battle, I would sometimes begin to cry. My mother would come in and sit on my bed, singing softly and stroking my forehead until I fully capitulated. Of course, I always woke up the next morning rested and ready for another day, so one would think that my fear would slowly subside as time went on, but it didn't, not until I graduated from my first bedtime prayer to the Lord's Prayer at the age of seven or eight. It was only years later, when I had to teach my first child,

Matthew, a bedtime prayer that I suddenly understood where that extreme fear of sleep had originated for me as a child. It was in that prayer:

Now I lay me down to sleep;
I pray the Lord my soul to keep.
Angels guard me through the night,
And keep me safe 'til morning bright.
If I should die before I wake,
I pray the Lord my soul to take.
Amen.

It was in the prayer the whole time—a prayer that had originated long ago, and in a different world, where infant and child mortality rates were sky high, and the death of a child was a fairly common thing. It was with Matthew that I vowed to myself that I would never teach that archaic, scary bedtime prayer to any of my children.

When Christopher in turn climbed into his bunk that night and slid himself down between the covers, the two of us said the special prayer that has become our custom at night:

Father, I am glad that you never cease to love me,
Whether it be day or night, sun or stars above me.
Now another day is done, and the quiet night is here;
Give me sweet, refreshing sleep, and keep the angels near.
And when the morning comes again, help me to greet the day
With happy thoughts and happy smiles,
and guard me at my play.

Amen.

"I suppose that from now on we should pray for God to keep us safe from illusions and shadows, too," Chris said when we were finished.

"Absolutely," I said, stepping up on the edge of the lower bunk so that I could give him a kiss and a big, long hug. "You seem to be feeling better about death lately," I said. "Have our conversations helped a little?"

"Yes," he said, the two of us still locked in a hug. "I feel a lot better about it, but I still think about it sometimes."

"You wouldn't be normal if you didn't," I said.

"I wouldn't?" he said, sounding a little surprised.

"No. We all think about it from time to time, and it scares us sometimes."

"Even you?"

197

"Once in a while, even me," I said, breaking the hug so I could see his face. "Just because I'm a minister doesn't mean that I'm not scared of death sometimes, too. Did you know that even Jesus was scared of dying?"

"*Jesus* was?" he echoed, incredulous.

"Yes," I said. "In the Garden of Gethsemene before he was arrested, Jesus prayed and prayed to God that he wouldn't have to die the next day because he was so scared. He was right in the middle of that big huge shadow. But the more he prayed, the more God brought him out of that shadow, and by the time the soldiers came to arrest him, Jesus was strong again, and brave enough to go with them, because he knew that even though he died, everything was going to be just fine in the end. Those soldiers gave him a real hard time; they beat him and whipped him and finally crucified him, but three days after he was killed, Jesus started appearing to his friends and telling them that he was okay, didn't he?"

"Yes," Chris said with a smile.

"Well, everything is going to be okay with you and me, too, no matter what ever happens to us," I assured him as I turned off the light. "Good night."

"Good night, Dad," he said. "I love you."

"I love you more," I answered, pulling the door shut. From the inside of Christopher's room I could hear a giggle. I pushed the door open again and said, "Was that an illusion, or did I hear somebody laughing in here?"

"It was real," he said, "because *I* love *you* more."

"That's impossible," I said. "I love you all the way to Jupiter and back again."

"Well, I love you all the way to Pluto and back," he countered.

"Gee whiz, that's a lot. I guess you win. Good night."

"Good night," came the garbled reply, accompanied by a yawn.

After everyone was tucked into bed, I went outside and began to make my way slowly down the path to the dock. I had left the keys in the boat earlier in the evening and wanted to remove them for the night. It has been many years since I last took a flashlight with me at night on that path; the exact position of each rock, tree root, and depression has been etched in my mind since childhood. On this particular night the moon was low in the sky and nearly full, its pale light bathing the lake and raising up eerie shadows along its bank and in the woods. Despite my familiarity with the path, I stumbled a couple of times on the way as moon shadows deceived my eyes into seeing obstacles where there were none, and not seeing the ones that were there. Halfway down, I stopped trying to watch the path, and raised my eyes, fixing my sight on the objective; with the dock in sight at the edge of the lake, I could easily judge my relative position on the path, and my feet took their direction from memory, solid footing achieved with each successive step.

Approximately ten feet from the final turn, beyond which lay the ramp leading straight out to the dock, strange noises in the wild blueberry bushes next to the ramp stopped me right where I was. There was a low chortling sound, followed by a high-pitched squeal and some rustling of the bushes. The first impression that came to my mind was that an owl had swooped down and grabbed a chipmunk, and was in the process of dispatching it before carrying it back to its nest. I slowly walked forward, straining my eyes in the moonlight to see what was going on. As I approached the bushes, the noises repeated themselves: a low chortling, another high-pitched squeal, and then the bushes in front of me started rustling violently, as if the owl and its hapless prey were about to tumble right out of the bushes at my feet. I turned and ran back up the path about twenty feet, not wanting to end up in the middle of this conflict, my heart pounding in my chest from the rush of adrenaline triggered by my fear.

As I turned around and watched again from a distance, another sound was added to the previous mix: more chortling, squealing, rustling, and now the distinct sound of splashing, as the struggle descended into the shallows. Now that the combatants were in the lake, I felt more confident about approaching again. I walked slowly forward, anxious to see how an owl and a chipmunk would fare in the water together. I reached the end of the path, turned and stepped onto the ramp, my eyes immediately scouring the water below. What they saw there in the full light of the moon made my mind reel; I was gripped with a raw terror which was absolutely unlike anything I have ever felt before. Every voice of sanity within me was shouting that what I was looking at could not exist, but there it was, clearly visible in the moonlight: silent now and alone, presumably because it had prevailed in the struggle and swallowed its prey, a huge black serpent was swimming into the lake. At least four inches in diameter, its glistening head and the first twelve inches of its body were leading the way on the surface, and two feet behind that, another eight-inch section arched above the surface.

Before my mind had even processed all that my eyes had fed it, I sprang reflexively backwards, turned in mid-air, and then stumbled over a large root that crossed the path, and I fell to my knees. Springing to my feet, I raced back up the path a short way and stopped, my mind frantically trying to make sense of what I had just seen in the water, my heart pounding in my head, my lungs sucking in air as if I had just run flat-out for a full mile. There were harmless black water snakes that we saw from time to time in the water, but they did not begin to approach the size of this monster, and this one had first been up in the bushes. I ran back almost to the dock ramp, where some of our water equipment was stored. Feeling my way along the ground in the darkness, I picked up the largest fishing net we had, and then realized that even it was not big enough to catch this giant killer. I picked up another net in my other hand; no, even two would not do the job. *And what would it do to me*, I wondered with a shudder, *if I did catch it?* I looked back toward the dock just as the hideous thing swam around the side of our boat toward open water.

It couldn't do me any harm now, I thought, so I ran to the ramp and all the way out to the end of our dock, where I crouched, breathless, heart-beat thudding in my ears so loudly that it was all I could hear, eyes glued to the stern of our boat, waiting to see the monstrosity from a closer vantage point as it rounded the stern. Finally, the head emerged, then the hump further back. I had no camera, so I had to observe and remember every single detail of its appearance in order to describe it to others later, yet I knew that no one would ever believe me.

No more than three seconds later I rolled over on my side, my body limp, giddy relief washing

through me in waves. The sense of relief was overwhelming, although it was soon joined by another sensation, that of feeling foolish; for it was now clear that what I had taken for an attacking owl, and then a monster-sized serpent, was actually two little muskrats. They had been playing in the bushes, most likely after a meal of mussels at the water's edge, where they break open the shells on the rocks. Now, one following the other, gliding effortlessly through the moonlit water, they headed across the lake to their den.

I sat on the end of the dock and watched them until they disappeared in the distance. My laughter echoed back to me from the hills across the lake as I remembered what my son had said just minutes earlier: "I suppose that from now on we should pray for God to keep us safe from illusions and shadows . . ."

"You have a bizarre sense of humor," I shouted to the Creator, directing my gaze to the stars above. The waves lapping the shore suddenly sounded like peals of laughter, coming at me from all directions. Beside me in the water, little specks of light were dancing atop the waves. And I, the most recent target of a divine practical joke, lay back on the dock smiling, awash in moonlight, savoring the sheer wonder of it all.

EPILOGUE

A solitary loon floats the waters of the lake. The sky and water are gray today, so the bird's plumage of stark black and white vaults out from its bland surroundings. The alternating checkered feathering is apparently painted by the hand of a master, so precisely sharp are its boundaries and ordering. Cocky young drake, he glides through the water, pausing momentarily to raise his left wing up, folded, while he thrusts his narrow, sharp beak into the space below to nibble and scratch. Gliding a little farther, his head and most of his long neck under water the whole time, he suddenly stops and lifts his head up high, turning it to look in all directions. The head and neck disappear again, straight down, tail feathers pointing straight up for the merest fraction of a second, after which he totally disappears in a silent plunge through the water's surface.

Some thirty seconds later, he emerges about twenty-five yards distant, snaking his neck up and down as it completes the swallowing of a small white perch. Every couple of minutes his neck straightens, periscoping his head up, and out of his mouth comes a long, haunting call that echoes off the hills to the west and returns a distant reply. There is no response to his call because he is the only loon here. The picture of perfect grace, his rounds of the lake continue. Another few minutes and the loon will offer up another call, hoping to hear the answering cry of one of his parents or siblings. At close range, his eyes reveal their haunting crimson hue. If the sun were out, striking them at just the right angle, they would appear as if illuminated by a fiery glow from within.

The sun is not out today, however. It shines less and less as each successive day becomes shorter. It is December, and ice defines the perimeter of the shoreline. This solitary young male was born later in the season than the rest of the brood, and when the time came for loons to leave the lake, he was not mature enough to fly. Healthy and strong for the moment, he will perish soon after the ice encroaches in from the edges and covers completely the surface of the water. He will begin to starve without access to the fish that swim below; moreover, he will not be able to wing his way to more hospitable climes even if he should feel that mysterious instinctive urge, for loons can only take off from water while it is still in the liquid state, where their large webbed feet paddle them along at speeds faster than they can walk on a solid surface. On the ice, they can manage nothing more than a rudimentary waddle, which is not even close to the escape velocity required to leave our lake. Oblivious to his impending doom, the loon glides motionless through the frigid waters, gradually approaching the northern shore.

As the bird crosses an invisible boundary, a woman, bundled against the windy winter chill, moves slowly and carefully down the outside steps of her little house near the shore. She makes her way to the edge of the lake, where she stops and lifts her head, her bright blue eyes riveted to the loon and her face taking on an air of determination. She takes in a full breath of Maine winter air and lets out a robust, clear call that sweeps out over the lake and echoes off the western hills, returning a second later; she intended to mimic the periodic cry of the loon. He does not respond, though he does cast a curious eye toward the woman. Confident she now has his attention, the woman begins to speak. In an authoritative British accent, she explains the seriousness of his predicament, and urges him to "Go find Mum and Dad; follow them. You must fly, dear creature," she implores him. Then, waving her outstretched arms up and down like wings, she intones the mantra over and over again as she does so: "Fly . . . fly . . . fly . . . " The doomed bird changes course, heading back out into the lake, away from this curious woman, who lets out another call with the hope of turning him around. When he does not, she begins to sing the most beautiful song, as soothing as a Celtic blessing when heard from a distance. Its resonant tones spread out over the lake, blessing the unfortunate loon and sanctifying everything else in its path: a soft blanket of love and comfort gently laid over a nearly frozen lake. Pulling her hood back over her head and turning, she leans forward to watch her steps, making her way slowly back to the house. Her long winter coat clings tightly to her body in the wind. Tomorrow she will again wait for the stranded loon to swim by her house, and she will make another attempt to help him come to his senses and fly away to safety. The woman recently lost her only son, a young man in his forties, and she and her husband have thought of nothing else since his death.

My mother recounts this story to me over the telephone, as she and my dad are now permanent residents at the lake in their retirement. The story's arrival is timely, for Christopher has just attended a memorial service at school for a beloved young English teacher, Mr. Sergeant, who died shortly after being diagnosed with a brain tumor. I have been concerned about Christopher, wondering if his teacher's untimely death or the memorial service has stirred up within him the same uncertainties and fears that hounded him the previous summer.

He and I sit together in the evening stillness, and I tell him the story of the stranded loon and the woman who has braved the snow and ice each day to call and talk and wave and sing him up into the sky.

"What do you think is going on here," I ask him, "when that beautiful, healthy loon will have lived for only one summer and autumn, and then die?"

"Dad," he says with a wisdom in his voice beyond his years, "the fact is that whether it is Mr. Sergeant or that loon, God made both of them, and I guess that God can take either of them back whenever he wants to."

"Sure he can," I agree, "But most people live longer than Mr. Sergeant, and most loons have a lot more time than the one up at the lake has been given."

"But there's a *reason*, Dad," he insists. "Right now I'm not sure why Mr. Sergeant had to leave so early. But what I do know is that up in Maine,

God sent the woman's son back to earth in that loon's body for a little while just so he could try and get his mother back to living again." Pause. "Oh . . . I guess that brings us back to reincarnation again, doesn't it?"

"Actually, no. It doesn't," I say.

"It doesn't?"

"No. I mean, most people who teach about reincarnation say that it works the other way. In other words, people don't come back as worms or as fish or even as birds, because it goes in the other direction. You grow as you go, so worms could come back as fish, and maybe fish as birds, but not the other way," I explain.

"Oh," he says, sounding a little bewildered. "Then what can people ever become? Supermen and superwomen? Angels?"

"I don't know exactly how it is all supposed to work," I say. "But I don't think we're talking about reincarnation here. What I'm really interested in right now is what you think about people who die suddenly after living what seems to us a pretty short life. What do you think that means?"

"Well," Christopher says, "even those people who live for over a hundred years, what's that to God?"

"What?"

"Think about it, Dad. Whether you live for one year or a hundred years, that's like nothing to God, because he has lived forever, and he's always going to be just living forever, so to him one hundred years is nothing at all. He doesn't care how long we live."

"He doesn't care?" I ask.

"He cares about us," he clarifies. "But I mean he doesn't think that someone has had a good life or a bad life by how many years they live, because how ever many it is, all those years are still nothing to him. They're really nothing to us, too; we just don't know it yet. What God actually cares about is how we act while we're here."

"Yes," I say. "I think you're right about that."

After a few moments of silence, he shoots me a quizzical look and says, "Dad, I understand what you said about reincarnation and how it's supposed to work, but I want to know if you think that God is powerful enough, if he wanted to, to send the lady's son back to her in that loon's body for a little while."

"Christopher," I respond, "I believe that God can do anything he wants to do. So I would have to say that yes, God could send her son back in that loon if he wanted to, but I don't really think that's what is going on here."

213

His eyes immediately widen, and he looks straight at me and speaks with renewed confidence. "Dad, I'm absolutely sure that loon was really her son; or maybe her son just had God send the loon for him. But once he got her to come out and start singing again, he just went back up to heaven and was happy, because he knew his mom was going to be okay. That's the only reason the loon was there. God will take good care of the loon when he dies, just like He has taken good care of the woman's son."

Christopher is distracted suddenly, fumbling with his pants pocket. He retrieves a playing card from the deck of a magical game in which the forces of light and truth battle the forces of darkness and evil. "By the way, Dad," he says as he hands it to me, "I've been meaning to ask you what you think of this quote. I really like it a lot."

On the face of the card is an angelic female figure in the moonlight wearing layers of shimmering white gossamer. Below the figure is an inscription:

The answer to life should never be death;
It should always be more life,
Wrapped tight around us in layers,
Like precious silks.

214

"That's absolutely beautiful," I tell him, capti-vated by the power of the words. "What a won-derful quote."

"Don't you think the world would be a much better place if everyone carried this card around with them and looked at it a few times each day?"

"Yes, Christopher; I certainly do. Thank you."

He wraps his arms around me then, and for a timeless moment we pause: two fellow sojourn-ers locked in an awesome bear hug that will most assuredly continue even when both of us have left this world and journey on anew.

Always more life . . .

Always.

ENDNOTES

1. *Life Prayers*. New York: HarperCollins, 1996, 331.
2. *Earth Prayers*. New York: HarperCollins, 1991, 325.
3. Kahlil Gibran, *The Prophet*. New York: Alfred A. Knopf, 1981, 80.
4. James R. Mills, *Poems of Inspiration from the Masters*. Grand Rapids, MI: Fleming H. Revell Company, 1979.
5. *Life Prayers*. New York: HarperCollins, 1996, 345.
6. Ibid., 330.
7. Ibid., 90.